Margo Wood

A Prairie Chicken Goes To Sea

A country girl experiences exciting and often humorous adventures with her husband while boating. Follow Margo as she deals with the death of her husband, decides to continue boating (often single-handed) and carry on the task of expanding and updating *Charlie's Charts* cruising guides.

Make your dreams live –
Margo Wood

CHARLIE'S CHARTS
Division of Polymath Energy Consultants Ltd.

National Library of Canada Cataloguing in Publication Data
Wood, Margo.
    A prairie chicken goes to sea

ISBN 0-9686370-2-7

1. Wood, Margo. 2. Wood, Charles E. (Charles Edward), 1928-1987.
3. Women sailors--Canada--Biography. 4. Cartographers--Canada--
Biography. 5. Voyages and travels. I. Title.
GV810.92.W66A3 2002   797.1 092   C2002-910300-2

Also by Margo Wood
Charlie's Charts of Costa Rica
Charlie's Charts of the United States Pacific Coast - co-author: Charles Wood

Edited by Helen McFadden
Design and layout by Christine Stefanitsis

Published by:
CHARLIE'S CHARTS
Division of Polymath Energy Consultants Ltd.
P.O. Box 45064, Ocean Park RPO
Surrey, BC V4A 9G4 CANADA

Tel/Fax: (604) 531-6292
Web site: charliescharts.com

PRINTED IN CANADA

For

Devereau and Charmian

Acknowledgements

I wish to thank Helen McFadden for her persistence in encouraging me to write this autobiography. Her painstaking efforts helped to make my writing worthy of publication. As children, Devereau and Charmian, often quizzed me about my "other life," and they continue to show interest in our family's past; I thank them for their curiosity.

A debt of gratitude is due to Maurice Brager for his steadfast support and encouragement for over 10 years. He has been a good sport in everything from riding elephants in Thailand and camels in Morocco to driving impossible primitive roads in Costa Rica, painting *Ern's* hull and acting as *Charlie's Charts'* skeleton staff when I go sailing. I thank him for giving me a relaxed base of operations and the space I need for my various ventures.

A special thank you is due to Christine Stefanitsis for her patience and much needed sense of humor while coaching me through the tangled web of desktop publishing. I am grateful to Carol Hasse, John Guzzwell and John Neal for their kind words.

A particular note of appreciation is due to Tristan Reiner for her book, *Your Life as Story*. She made me think deeply about the experiences and patterns of my life that seemed at the time to be nothing short of floundering. Her book gave me the tools to write this narrative.

Contents

Charles and Margo

PREFACE – A Book is Born in Bottleneck Inlet

It was a glorious day. The trip from Oliver Cove, where I'd anchored overnight, had been perfect. As I approached Perceval Narrows, the early morning fog dissipated as if on command and wavelets sparkled in a channel that was guarded on either side by black reefs draped with glistening seaweed and kelp. Beyond the maze of low-lying rocky islets, the forested hills created an emerald backdrop where occasionally the odd weathered, gray snag stood out. Overhead, the cloudless sky was a bright blue against which gliding, arguing seagulls were painted.

My route took me through scenic, protected waters until passing into Finlayson Channel where the entrance to Bottleneck Inlet is located. I wanted to explore this inlet, for the chart showed it only as a narrow slit in the coast of Roderick Island off British Columbia's rugged west coast. The description in the official Sailing Directions was predictably brief and to the point, giving no hint of the dramatic atmosphere in this picturesque spot. The narrow entrance is shrouded on either side by towering evergreens and is easy to miss, so that cruisers transiting the area often bypass this hidden paradise. But as I crossed the threshold I felt as if I was about to enter a special sanctuary. *Ern* and I moved slowly, absorbing the mystical atmosphere before anchoring in the still, protected waters.

As is my habit when anchored alone in an isolated anchorage, I ate dinner in the cockpit and listened to some of my favorite tapes—the music of Mozart, Charlotte Church, Neil Diamond, and a magnificent Welsh Male Choir. The cove offered a spectacular scene as the long twilight faded and a half moon lit the inlet with a gentle glow. The dark gloom of the forested hills became outlined against a starry sky and all was reflected in the still waters of the cove. The air became cool, and

11

the cockpit seats grew damp with the evening dew. Just as I went below for the night the mournful cry of a lonely loon echoed across the water. Good night and peace to all.

The next morning, after planning my route and destination for the new day, I raised the anchor and left my idyllic spot. It was a fresh, sunny day and I had traveled for less than half an hour when suddenly I began to question my motive for moving on. Why was I leaving such a beautiful anchorage when I had over a month to reach my turn-around at Kitimat and the delta of the Kitlope River? What was the rush? I could find no good reason to continue, so I turned around and headed back to Bottleneck Inlet to soak up more of the joyful solitude of this breathtaking spot.

There in my meditation I thanked God for my good health and the opportunity to experience such beauty and peace at this time in my life. I thought of the many people my age who had resigned themselves to lives of monotony and boredom, and celebrated my good fortune in finding another way to live out my years. In my diary I started to reminisce, describing some of the memorable trips I'd had while cruising along the British Columbia coast. Before I knew it the day had passed and I was left with a notebook full of memories. The next day, content and rested, I left the anchorage, passed through Heikish Narrows and continued northbound through Graham Reach, until anchoring in fog-shrouded Khutze Inlet.

On my return to "civilization," the notebook joined a stack of logbooks and journals from previous trips. Then, several years later as I read some of these notes and I began to realize that the long road traveled from starting out as a non-swimming landlubber to eventually becoming a happy single-handed sailor might provide an interesting story. Although I hadn't made any headlines, the trails taken had been marked with both exhilaration and adversity—a life I wouldn't trade for a world of fame and fortune.

This narrative is the result, the true tale of events in the life of a person who wanted to live life to the full, come what may. The names of some people have been changed to protect their privacy.

Fortunately, along the way I married Charles, who had a similar attitude and had the courage to take me along with him on land and seafaring adventures filled with a kaleidoscope of experiences. At first I was reluctant to venture onto the ocean, but it offered unique opportunities, mental and physical challenges and the possibility for travel. Every trip was a learning experience, sometimes unnerving, sometimes humorous, always rewarding. Successive voyages became increasingly enjoyable, and steadily built my confidence. I began to believe in the boat and in our ability to safely handle it in varied conditions, and sailing became the fullest adventure of them all.

And out of this life together came, completely unplanned, the creation of cruising guides based on some of our boating experiences. Cruisers often ask how *Charlie's Charts* got started and how I've managed to continue publishing the guides since his death. Since *Charlie's* became the "Bible" for many cruisers, I was tempted to name this autobiographical effort, "*Life With a Legend and Beyond.*" Sadly, his life was cut short by a heart attack at the age of 59, and I was left alone to deal not only with the grief of his passing but also with the challenge of continuing to publish guides that were beginning to make a positive contribution to cruising in Pacific waters.

Recently, numerous women have expressed surprise (and have probably questioned my sanity) when they learn that this little white-haired old lady often cruises the coast single-handed. "Are you ALONE in that boat?" "Aren't you AFRAID?" "How do you do everything that needs to be done?" are frequent astonished queries. I want to answer these questions, and encourage anyone beginning to participate in boating as an adult to believe in themselves and persevere—it is possible to overcome trepidation and learn to enjoy boating. If I could overcome my insecurity, anyone can.

At the same time I would like to give a measure of hope to skippers with reluctant first mates by demonstrating that with patience, time and experience, novices can become competent boaters who take genuine pleasure in participating in a successful trip.

An additional outcome of this story may be to encourage those who have lost a partner to realize that life goes on, and it is possible to develop new interests or continue to enjoy experiences you once shared with a loved one. Certainly one must approach life in a different way now, but happiness and contentment are still possible. In my case, of course, losing Charles resulted in my continuing satisfying work as caretaker of his legacy, *Charlie's Charts,* revisiting the areas covered by the guides, collecting current information, updating editions and visiting with cruisers. This active symbol of our life together is a gift I continue to enjoy.

Bottleneck Inlet

1   In The Beginning . . . .

My father fled in panic from our tired looking homestead when my mother commenced the painful task of bringing me into the world. He struggled frantically into his heavy wool mackinaw jacket, pulled a sheepskin cap over his head, lit a kerosene hurricane lantern and raced to the barn. The dry, hard-packed snow gave a crisp squeak with every footstep and seemed to add a note of urgency, while the erratic swinging of the lantern flung wild and crazy patterns of light and dark in all directions. At last he reached the log barn where eight head of heavy draft horses were snuggly bedded down for the night. Trying not to pass on his nervous anxiety, he spoke in a low voice to Beauty and King as he buckled up their harness and led them out into the cold night air, where each breath created a cloudy puff. Their velvety ears twitched as he hitched them to a small, enclosed homemade sleigh. The team had never been taken out at night and they sensed that something unusual was afoot, but they dutifully responded to the usual commands until the lantern was extinguished and they were ready to go.

A full moon shining from a cloudless sky lit the scene with a brilliant white light, making the way clear. The gentle slopes of parkland faded into the distance in one direction, while on the other side clumps of willow and poplar marked a gully unfit for cultivation. A pair of coyotes let out mournful howls that were soon answered by faint responses off in the distance. Ignoring the beauty of the scene my father drove the team furiously on a faint track across the snow-covered field to a neighbor's farm about a mile away.

The house where my story begins

My mother had been left to her own resources from an early age and had developed a strong and self-reliant attitude that was often called on throughout her life. As it happened, she had chosen to become a nurse in her quest to make a living, and now her training and experience took over, and she dealt with the situation at hand. Fortunately it was an uncomplicated birth as I burst forth into the world. My father of course returned once the messy business was over, and our family was complete. What possessed Dad to abandon my mother at such a crucial time and flee to the home of a bachelor was a mystery he never explained. He always laughed off his actions and changed the subject! Only once in later years did Mom speak of this incredible night.

The year was 1934, in the midst of the depression, when the birth of another child—especially a girl—was not so much celebrated as simply tolerated. Thus I joined many other children born during the dirty 30's who were referred to as "accidents." My birth took place in a one-bedroom, uninsulated homestead in the Peace River country of northern Alberta where winter temperatures can drop as low as –44°C (–50°F). During the Great Depression our farm income was barely enough to pay for basic necessities, and the bank sent several letters threatening to seize the homestead if payment on a small loan was not made on time. For many years my parents struggled to hold onto the farm and provide necessities of life for the family. As in pioneering days, wheat harvested on the farm was ground into flour by a miller who was paid in kind, wild berries were canned and farm-grown vegetables were bottled or stored in a root cellar. We ate simple, filling fare.

During school years most of my clothing consisted of hand-me-downs from friends in Vancouver. Every year the arrival of the box of used clothing was greeted with keen anticipation. Nothing was wasted, as even impractical party dresses were cut up to begin a new life as cowboy shirts. The persistence and hard work of my parents eventually brought results and during the war they were able to pay off the onerous debt that had hung over their heads for many years. This quest to make a living and hold the farm allowed little room for "quality time with the family." Mom often confided to me how much she would like to take a holiday from the farm "just for a week or so to get away from all the hard work." They never did manage to leave the farm until it was finally sold, by which time they didn't have the strength, interest or energy to enjoy a holiday.

As a child oblivious to my parents' financial worries, I thoroughly enjoyed the variety of simple tasks that enabled me to participate in farm activities: feeding chickens, collecting eggs, filling the wood box, picking wild berries, herding the cow to the barn and milking her.

Activities for family members all centered on work to be done to raise livestock and grow crops as the seasons changed. As a youngster, I spent many hours riding the tractor alongside my father as he tilled the fields. Sometimes as a treat he let me steer the tractor while crossing wide spaces and finally, when I turned 13, he gave me a supreme vote of confidence by allowing me drive it alone. What a sense of power and independence! The dust, cool showers and cold winds mattered little as I drove the big McCormick-Deering for hours at a time plowing, harrowing or hauling other farm machinery.

There were other jobs that needed to be done, and riding a workhorse to herd cattle or horses to a new pasture also gave me a sense of control and freedom at an early age. I gloried in a feeling of oneness with animals and the surroundings so closely tied to nature. I pleaded for several years to have my own saddle horse, and Dad finally relented and purchased a spunky little sorrel mare that became my steady partner whenever I wasn't in school. The movie stars, Roy Rogers and Gene Autry were my heroes—I sang their songs, practiced their trick roping and imitated their every move. I would spend count-less hours riding along country roads, and developed a connection with nature and an appreciation for prolonged periods of silent thought. For as Will Rogers so aptly said, "A man in the country does his own thinking, but you get him into town and he soon will be thinking second-handed."

Even before I started to go to the one-room country school I developed a lust for travel and adventure that was initiated by a most unlikely source: Blue Ribbon Tea. The tea was inexpensive and tasty, but also each package contained a small envelope of canceled stamps from foreign countries. Until the end of World War II, money for toys was scarce. Somehow Mom always managed to put aside enough to have a few gifts under the Christmas tree, but these presents always had some practical use, with nothing left over for the luxury of a hobby. So the little packet of stamps with each pound of tea was a wondrous treasure. I studied each stamp, fascinated by the strange-looking people and places from far-away countries. A partially used school notebook was carefully labeled "Stamp Album" and the stamps were meticulously stuck on the pages with a paste made of flour and water. This stamp album was my treasure chest of dreams, for it opened the door to distant worlds that were impossibly remote and unreachable for a homesteader's daughter. The images of Chinese junks, exotic dancers and strange animals gave a focus for my imagination, planting the seeds of a desire for travel and adventure. The dream that one day I would find a way to escape from my isolated world was finally solidified while reading *After You, Marco Polo* by Jean Bowie Shor. This adventure-packed tale of her exciting trip helped to strengthen my determination still further.

Pals

Throughout my formative years, the gently rolling parkland of the Peace River country of northern Alberta was considered the "back of beyond." Towering grain elevators marked the small towns that were linked by dirt roads or steam-powered trains, and sometimes even both. Farms were few and far between, and feelings seemed to run high—either you were on friendly terms with your neighbors or, because of some simple disagreement in the past, you would steadfastly have nothing to do with them. Fortunately, we were on great terms with our nearest neighbors, and we regularly visited each other.

Some of my fondest memories are of times when, bound for home following a visit, I would ride my horse for an hour or so over moonlit country roads. In the summer, the swaying fields of grain foretold similar patterns of the wind on moonlit waves I was to see many years later at sea. In the winter, the snow-covered fields reflected the moon's bright light, and the shadows it cast were sharp and clear. In these northern latitudes the dancing Northern Lights crackled and snapped as they added a brilliant curtain of constantly changing colors to the magnificent scene. There was an almost hypnotizing effect of the undulating lights as they danced about the sky. When I look back at that period of my life I appreciate the quiet solitude of the country life that gave me time and space to think, to dream and gradually, to plan. Now I realize why the seemingly very different life of the lone seafarer has a sense of nostalgia to it.

The next stage of my life found me leaving the rolling landscape of the north to attend university in Edmonton, where I was one of first students from the "backwoods" to progress beyond high school. Then, I lived two separate lives, jumping through the hoops of the social life as a university student yet happily returning during vacations to the peace and quiet of country life. It was the 1950s, a time when a farm girl was expected to marry a farm boy, produce a sizable brood of offspring and play the role of a dutiful country wife. I had other plans.

During my freshman year I was dreadfully homesick and painfully aware of my lack of sophistication. I tried to fit in with the social scene, but soon realized that I wasn't meant to follow the sorority crowd. Knowing the rate of dropouts in first-year university I was anxious about the possibility of failure. And of course I was well aware of the many neighbors who were watching my progress, equally ready to celebrate my success or to condemn my failure with a knowing nod of the head and a comment that, "She should'a married old Tom's boy instead of bein' so high an'mighty an' goin' off to the big city."

While attending university, doubts persisted as to whether it was right for me to place such a large financial burden on my parents. When the moon shone through the window of the women's residence where I lived my thoughts often turned to my home in the north, and I consoled myself with the realization that it was shining just as brightly on the rolling countryside there, on my parents and on my horse. I pretended that it was a silent link to my other life and in some strange way this thought helped me to find strength to carry on, persevere and succeed.

Summer job in Jasper, Alberta

21

During university summer vacations, my love of the outdoors led me to the mountain towns of Banff and Jasper where I worked as a chambermaid, waitress and office clerk. Every day off I would spend hitchhiking to a trailhead and exploring the wonders of these two spectacular National Parks. These were exciting times, scrambling up cliffs and mountain trails to discover scenic wonders in a stunning mountain playground, while catching glimpses of a wonderful variety of wildlife. I was beginning to expand my horizons and starting to fulfill my dreams.

As graduation approached, I planned to pay off my debts, and then save enough money to finance a trip around the world, supplementing my savings by working along the way. With this in mind I took my first job, teaching business education at Crescent Heights High School in Calgary for two years while I planned my great adventure. Summers would find me hiking and rock climbing; weekends in the winter often were spent skiing, all the time, honing and feeding my dreams. Norma, a friend from university days, shared my ambition and was keen to accompany me on this odyssey. We planned to begin the trip in 1957, heading first to New Zealand then to Australia. We searched for people to advise us on economical travel abroad, for this was long before there were publications like the *Lonely Planet* or the wealth of travel guides that are available today. We did know that by the time we had reached Europe our savings would be depleted and our travel would be on less than a shoestring! The school secretary knew of my concerns and suggested that I come to dinner to meet an engineer from Scotland who had frequently traveled on a limited budget to climb the Alps in France and Switzerland. This person was Charles Edward Wood.

Charles had been born in Sagaing, Burma in 1928. His father was an English civil engineer and his mother was a beautiful woman with a potpourri of races in her background —English, Portuguese, Burmese and who knows what else came from the roots of early explorers, traders and sailors who visited Burma during the age of discovery. When the Japanese overran Burma in 1941, British subjects and their families fled to southern ports attempting to escape the invading forces. As news came of the speedy invasion they had only a few hours to pack whatever they could carry and flee. Charles, his father, mother and brother were overtaken by the Japanese forces and incarcerated in a makeshift compound in southern Burma. There, incredibly, an elderly Japanese jailer felt sorry for the family of innocent victims of war, and deliberately left a gate open through which they were able to escape. Dashing to the harbor, they were able to scramble aboard the last British ship departing for England. Penniless and torn from the only home the family had ever known, they began a new life in England as refugees. Charles eventually went to Glasgow, where he enrolled in the University of Glasgow Certificate Program for Engineering Design at night while working during the day at Alexander Stephens and Sons Shipbuilders.

His love of the outdoors led him to mountaineering, and he spent most weekends and holidays mountain climbing in Scotland and the French and Swiss Alps. His skill and reputation as a mountaineer developed to such a level that he was short-listed for the British Himalayan expedition of 1955. However, when he wasn't chosen for the final team he emigrated to Canada, along with two of his Scottish climbing buddies, with the intention of planning for their own low-budget Himalayan expedition. However, while skiing in Banff he suffered a serious fall, injuring his knee so badly that plans for that climbing expedition were terminated.

During my first meeting with Charles, I was fascinated to hear of the extensive climbing trips he had taken in the Alps and I was surprised to learn that the worn-down remains of mountains in Scotland offered many challenging climbs, especially in winter when ice climbing was popular. He described the widespread Youth Hostel system in Europe and the mountain huts available to back-packers and hikers. I

23

thought he was a little long-winded in his explanations of cost cutting for travelers, but I appreciated the information. It definitely was not 'love at first sight' though we shared some common interests and I enjoyed his sense of humor and the wealth of knowledge he freely shared.

Mountaineering in the French Alps

We took many trips to Banff, Jasper and the Kananaskis, climbing and photographing wildlife and mountain scenery. Whether we were hiking to glorious alpine meadows or climbing new routes on un-named mountains, we were in our element. We became fond of each other and made long-term plans to renew our friendship on my return. However, my long-awaited adventure with Norma was terminated when the number of deaths resulting from the Australian Flu Epidemic of 1957-8 prompted her to change her mind. My dream of travel came to a screeching halt; it did not occur to me to embark on such a venture alone.

Charles and I began to see more of each other and our mutual affection grew. Until this time the thought of marriage was not a priority in my life. I had seen too much sadness at home as my hard-working parents struggled to make a living. More importantly the lack of understanding, respect and love shown by my father for my mother always created a pall over the family atmosphere. For me as a teen-ager, the icy mood surrounding my parents became oppressive and I longed to escape. When I did consider the concept of marriage, it seemed as if the best choice for me was to become a "career girl," enjoy mixed company, but proceed to go my own way in life independently. However, Charles was different from other men—his sense of humor, his courage to reach for the stars, his creativity, his wonderful mind and our shared enthusiasm for adventure—all these had led to strong feelings of attraction that opposed my independent plans.

My parents hated Charles because of his indeterminate racial background. My mother feared that by associating with him I would suffer abuse similar to what she had known as a result of her one-quarter Native Indian background and that our children would be ostracized. My father joined in these strong negative feelings and refused to meet Charles, eventually threatening, "I'll shoot him if he ever sets foot on the farm." The next day, his hunting rifle leaned on the wall just behind his favorite chair. For two months I tried to encourage them to get to know and appreciate the man that I loved. They refused. Shattered, I packed my bags and left my home, praying that they would reconsider and not follow through with their threat to disown me. I returned to Calgary and resumed teaching. Charles and I made plans to marry in the spring, take a prolonged trip to Great Britain and Europe and make our home in Vancouver.

I sent notification of the day of our proposed wedding to my parents and kept hoping that I would learn of a change of heart on their part. A week before our wedding a large parcel arrived. *Was this a wedding present to show that they still loved me and wished me well in my new life? Please, God, let it be.* Optimistically anticipating reconciliation, I ripped off the tape and tore open the box. A six-tined pitchfork stabbed my heart and soul! There before me was a collection of all the presents I had ever given my parents, from a circus booklet drawn in primary school to the most recent birthday gift, a china cream and sugar set modeled after Anne Hathaway's cottage. I was devastated.

Then my perspective changed, and I realized the depth of the hurt they must be feeling to make such a harsh, cold decision. I had given my choice serious thought, and though deeply pained and hurt to my very core I, too, had made a decision I was prepared to stand by. This cruel standoff made me even more determined to see that our marriage was a success. I knew in my heart that I had made the right decision, resigned myself to their forceful handling of our difference of opinion and attempted to close the door on my family past. I resolutely looked to the future with optimism and anticipation, although I had no idea of the twists and turns that life had in store for me!

And so, Charles and I were married in the spring of 1958. We made a down payment on a fire engine red Triumph TR3 sports car which we took delivery of in England, and spent six months holidaying in Britain and Europe. I was able to meet his parents and I also managed to satisfy some of my wanderlust before we returned to Canada. We settled in Vancouver, where he attended the University of British Columbia and I took a teaching position to finance his studies.

Honeymoon in Banff, Alberta

2 DELOS

Like many idealists, Charles had always dreamed of owning a sailboat and cruising to distant sunny shores. I shared his longing to travel, but not the means of getting there! I did not share his interest in boating, for my image of the ocean was a collage of the paintings of shipwrecked vessels and drowning sailors, faces full of terror as they prayed for deliverance from tempestuous seas. Moreover, I was a confirmed non-swimmer, and I had no desire to learn for the lake adjacent to the farm had been rimmed with green scum and one only had to dip a foot in the cold water for a few minutes to attract a bevy of revolting blood suckers. No, I was not a good candidate for a sailing partner. However, we were newly married, we were in love and I wanted to show Charles that I was a like-minded adventurer who had what it took to face any challenge. Besides, he tempted me with the idea that one day we could sail around the world. My dream resurfaced, adventure beckoned and I was hooked.

For several weeks we looked at a variety of boats that were for sale. We needed one large enough to provide me with a feeling of security. The idea of being on a vessel with water just inches away was so unsettling and foreign to me. Eventually we came across an affordable 30-foot yawl, a no-frills boat of indeterminate age and design, named after a Greek Island. Her down-to earth accommodation seemed luxuriously spacious when compared with the two-person mountaineering tent where we had spent many a night as we toured Europe. The wood burning stove in the galley promised to heat the main cabin, and the prospect of cozy nights in peaceful anchorages succeeded in blinding us to her many flaws. For one thing, the large cockpit provided a spacious area for entertaining guests on a sunny day but it drained into the bilge, making for an unsafe vessel in rough weather. But to our untrained eyes her recently painted plywood decks appeared to indicate a vessel that had been well maintained. The owner assured us *Delos* was a dry boat and we had nothing to fear. Though she was not a thing of beauty, we could afford her, as the owner had magnanimously agreed to take our shiny red Triumph TR3 in part payment.

Later *Delos* became a constant reminder of how gullible we had been and how much we had to learn not only about boats but also about people keen to sell something they no longer wanted. We had been impressed by the fact that the owner was an ex-Commodore of a yacht club. He showed us photographs of himself as Commodore, taking the salute during the annual sail past; he showed his family enjoying sailing, fishing and good times. A well-known, successful businessman, he wined and dined us in his magnificent waterfront home and we believed every word he said. We agreed to pay the grand sum of $3,300, and declined to have her surveyed when he assured us that a survey was money thrown away. "She's as solid as a rock—the surveyor won't find a thing wrong with her. Spend your money on something worthwhile." He saw us coming and we paid the price for our naiveté.

Delos was our first training ship, for each time we took her out for a sail we learned more lessons from the school of experience. With Peter Heaton's book, *Learning to Sail* in hand, we studied the section on how to handle the sails and tiller on each point of sail. Our first venture away from the dock was to the protected waters of Howe Sound near Vancouver where we anchored in quiet West Bay. For over an hour we tried in vain to sail her out of the bay, but finally gave up and motored back to the marina. Charles kept assuring me that he had sailed with friends in Scotland and that handling the boat was no problem, there just wasn't enough wind. I took him at his word and blindly followed along, believing he knew what he was doing and his wordy explanation was valid. What a typical man, he was bluffing, talking a good line, entirely based on theory! I was oblivious to the fact that we were the only vessel in the water with a captain and crew who had to refer to a book merely to sail out of the bay.

Delos in Pirate's Cove

Later, we realized that there were several reasons why our attempts to sail were unsuccessful: the rigging was not tuned, the shapeless canvas mainsail and stretched Egyptian cotton jib had little drawing power, and with our ineffective timing it was impossible to get enough way on to tack. *Delos* was a heavy vessel and it took a fair breeze to make her move along.

Slow as *Delos* was, I inadvertently reduced her passage through the water still further. I discovered that by shifting the tiller a certain way I could bring the mast to a vertical position and the boat would stop heeling. It made me feel safe to know that I could do something to prevent the boat from tipping over! Charles was very patient with my unwitting hindrance to our progress.

Though sunny skies and good sailing breezes in the Strait of Georgia were frequent that first summer we were boat owners, it was still a stressful time for me. My anxiety at the prospect of venturing out on the water was so intense that every weekend we went boating I suffered from stomach cramps. Those visions of shipwrecked sailors kept recurring! However, not wanting to disappoint Charles by letting on that I was petrified at the thought of boating, I put on a brave front and pretended to be keen to accompany him on these weekly trips. Almost every weekend found us either working on the boat or going for a sail, but how I silently rejoiced when Charles declared the weather unsuitable for sailing!

Though I had no experience caring for wood, I soon began to enjoy the results of hours of work, sanding weathered mahogany and oak and seeing the clear grain reappear, cleaning the surface with a tack rag, applying varnish and then seeing the rich glow of the shining, finished product. Looking back, I realize now that I probably enjoyed refinishing the boat's woodwork because it meant that we would be tied to the dock as long as work had to be done!

There was so much to learn, and since I had not prepared myself for this new chapter in my life by reading books about sailing and cruising I found the marine vocabulary confusing. There were inconsistencies that did not make sense to me such as, how could we be safe "in the lee of an island" yet need to "give a lee shore plenty of offing?" I didn't "get it." Courses in sailing were non-existent, except to members of a yacht club with membership fees far beyond our financial state with Charles attending university and my salary as a teacher just sufficient to cover living expenses.

One day we took an acquaintance sailing. He was familiar with the lingo of boating, and he and Charles were enjoying a lively dialog using appropriate marine terms as we readied *Delos* for a day on the water. I was not involved in the conversation and was clearly the silent partner. Charles asked me to go below and get the battens, so without admitting my ignorance, I went below and started to stow gear and food for the day. A few minutes later he poked his head down the hatch and asked,

"Where are the battens?"

"I don't know what battens are so how can I find them?" I shot back, "Why don't you two speak English?"

Assuming the role of an instructor, in his most pedantic manner he painstakingly explained that they were the thin wooden slats that helped to give shape to the mainsail. Without saying a word, I promptly passed them to him. Gradually my marine vocabulary grew, and each time we went boating I learned a few more things about the boat and how to handle it. Ever so slowly I started to develop a little more confidence in the idea of being afloat.

Reluctant first mate

Charles had warned me that weather conditions could sometimes change suddenly and that I could help by keeping an eye out for a squall line. When such a black, threatening line of clouds was approaching I was to alert him immediately, so that we could "reduce sail to avoid a knock-down." His description of a knock-down, with the boat suddenly flung broadside ninety degrees and lying on her side in the water, was all that I needed to add another element of fear to my adventures. My vivid imagination promptly shifted into gear, and this prospect impressed me to the extent that even on sunny days with fluffy fair-weather cumulous clouds I was constantly on the lookout for the dreaded squall line to raise its ugly head out of the blue. In our years of cruising we were fortunate never to experience such a situation, but I developed a keen weather eye as a result of his comments.

My progress as crew was dreadfully slow, but Charles was very patient—much more so than in later years. On one occasion in that first summer he thought my long-hoped-for advance on the learning curve was beginning to show some promise. We were returning from a sail in the Strait of Georgia under power since the wind had died, and we were about to cross the path of a British Columbia ferry known for its wicked, sharp wake. I began to fuss about how close we were to this behemoth whose bow wave seemed to me like a breaking tidal wave. Charles assured me that we had little to fear since we would be passing well clear of the monster, but this did little to ease my mind. The ferry passed astern of us and we gave it no more thought.

All of a sudden *Delos* was viciously tossed from side to side by the ferry's sharp wash, while from below came the clatter of the tea kettle being flung off the stove and a locker that had been insecurely latched emptying its contents onto the floor of the heaving cabin. Immediately I flew down the companionway as Charles beamed with pleasure thinking that I was rushing below to tidy up the cabin and put everything in its place. What a vain hope—tidying up was the last thing that entered my mind; the mess could sink with the boat! What a disappointment for him, as his next view was of a distraught woman spluttering and scolding, clambering into the cockpit, struggling into a life jacket and hanging on to the coaming for dear life. In recounting the incident to friends he usually ended by laughing, "The biggest insult of all was that she didn't even bother to bring up a life jacket for me!"

The last trip of the summer found us crossing the Strait of Georgia for a one-week cruise of the Gulf Islands, about 20 miles distant. It was our first overnight cruising experience and it was idyllic as we meandered through the chain of islands to set the hook in peaceful anchorages where we were often the only boat. This was at a time before the boating population had exploded and decimated the clam and oyster beds, so we were able to find a tasty meal ashore for the taking, or supply the larder with fresh-caught salmon whenever we wished. At night, the sparkle of phosphorescence dripped off the ends of the oars like tiny jewels and as the dinghy glided over the water it lit a shining path that thrilled me with childish delight. Similarly, the marine life that included killer whales, dolphins and pulsating translucent white jellyfish, gave me a sense of joy and appreciation. Then, at low tide there were the multi-colored sea anemone and starfish plastered on the rocks, in shades of purple, pink, orange and yellow, adding color to the scenic beauty of the marine environment.* I was beginning to enjoy boating and relax a little, for *Delos* had looked after us in the light airs of protected waters and had let me experience some of the gentle pleasures of life on the water.

However, this pleasant cruise had what seemed at the time to be an overly eventful ending, for as we returned to Vancouver, a gusty southeasterly wind picked up. Charles, thinking it best to forego a wet, slow beat with his unpredictable and nervous crew, started the motor in order to make port before nightfall. The seas built, and suddenly a series of three waves, noticeably larger than the others, came rushing toward us. I had never seen anything so threatening in my life. In the darkened evening sky the heaving water was so black and forbidding that I couldn't bear to look as the waves lunged toward our fragile vessel. I turned away in panic, my tongue a wad of felt in my mouth. I was terrified, but I kept silent and tried to tell myself that maybe we

It is sad to report that nowadays the prolific marine life of every kind is but a shadow of its former population as a result of pollution, over-fishing and lack of preservation of the environment.

would survive the ordeal. Charles told me to put a life jacket on and I complied, but it struck me as ominous.

"Do you think the boat is going to sink?" I asked.

"Some people jump overboard if they are frightened, and I just wanted to be sure you'd float," he curtly replied.

Good grief, jumping overboard was the last thing I was considering. But his precautions were justified, and to this day I remember how frightened and anguished I felt as we floundered slowly toward our moorage. Then suddenly the motor stopped.

"What's wrong now? I cried.

"The tank is empty. We'll just have to siphon some from the spare can, for it's too rough to pour it."

With no sails to steady the motion, the boat pitched and rolled uncomfortably in the sharp seas. Charles lifted the spare can of gasoline from a cockpit locker and handed a small rubber hose to me while he opened the can. Still terrified, but with new worries, I proceeded to suck the noxious fluid until the hose was full, but when I started to insert it into the fuel tank *Delos* lurched and the other end came out of the spare can.

"Damn, I have to do it again. This is a rotten cocktail," I grumbled.

"Don't get so much in your mouth."

"Thanks for the advice, just keep your end where it belongs!"

Taking a deep breath I sucked once more on the hose and this time we were able to siphon most of the spare fuel into the tank. Now all I could do was pray that the engine would start and we could get back to land. *Would this nightmare never end?*

We finally made port, well after nightfall. To my astonishment, there wasn't a breath of wind on shore, and we had survived what had appeared to be an attack by huge seas! This trip marked a turning point for me, as it did so much to build confidence in the seaworthiness of the boat in what I thought at the time were rough conditions. I felt that I could begin to relax in slightly stronger winds, and maybe eventually even really enjoy sailing.

Later, I also realized how insignificant the seas had actually been, but at the time everything had seemed so threatening. As our cruising career progressed we encountered heavier conditions, when each time new proof was needed of the vessel's capacity to stay afloat and of our ability to make proper decisions. When the season ended and *Delos* was warm and dry under her winter cover, we began to talk about how she could be modified for an offshore voyage.

Giving Delos a much needed face-lift

The following spring we put *Delos* up on the tidal grid to paint her bottom with copper paint. This was prior to the time when the toxicity of copper paint laced with arsenic was recognized as being harmful to marine life, but we took great care to prevent any from splashing our skin because it burned badly. It was at this time that my confidence in the boat took another leap forward for Charles had explained that the weight of the keel kept the boat from turning turtle when the force of the wind in the sails made the boat heel. Now, actually seeing the heavy iron keel I understood just how secure she was, and that there was no need for concern when the boat heeled to the wind. It was all beginning to make sense.

The weather turned warmer and we commenced to prepare her for a coat of paint, when suddenly our dreams came to an unexpected halt. While sanding painted surfaces in the cabin prior to applying a fresh coat I noticed some smooth, puffy areas around the portholes. Similarly, in the forward cabin there were several raised bubbles that had a peculiar hollow sound when gently tapped. At the same time, a suspicious indentation in the surface of the cockpit sides prompted Charles to prod with a sharp knife. To our dismay several patches of dry rot were discovered scattered about the boat, and our remodeling plans and dreams of faraway shores came to a sudden end. "We're not going offshore in a rotten boat, and with her design it's not worth trying to rebuild her to make a seaworthy vessel." Charles' tone was full of exasperation and disappointment. I voiced my opinion of the dishonesty of the yacht club ex-commodore, but we could only blame ourselves for not having had a survey done. We'd just have to sell her for what we could get and buy another boat. Next time, we resolved we would buy a solid, professionally designed and built vessel that had been thoroughly checked over.

To take our mind off our disappointment that the boat had let us down we once again turned to the mountains, and went to the quarry in North Vancouver to practice rock climbing. Here we met John Evans, a member of an expedition to Mount Waddington (13,104 ft.) that had been turned back by bad weather before reaching the summit. John was hoping to lead a team of six climbers with the intention of getting the first woman to the summit of the highest mountain in British Columbia, and he was looking for two more members for the team. We were happy to join the group, for our love of the mountains was a keen as ever and Charles' knee had completely healed. The plan was that the

38

final assault group would consist of four climbers, one being Elfrieda Pigout, a well-known climber who had already made a number of first ascents in the Rocky Mountains.

During our preparatory climbs with the group Charles became increasingly reluctant to continue with the expedition, and eventually we withdrew. Substitutes were found and the team headed for Mount Waddington, while we started to look for a new boat. On the day they were due to return from the mountain we received a phone call from the Royal Canadian Mounted Police, informing us that the entire party had been killed in an icefall during a night when they had set up camp on a glacier. It was a shock to realize how close we had been to such a disastrous turn of events. With heavy hearts we mourned their loss and realized how lucky we were to have escaped such an untimely death. We felt the time had come to decide—which would it be, mountaineering or sailing? After that close call, sailing seemed a much safer choice, even to me!

Although forced to sell *Delos* at a loss, we were fortunate to find someone who wanted her as a boat to tinker with, and we had no hesitation in telling him that she had plenty of tinkering potential! He had no impractical dreams about such a small investment, and both parties to the sale were satisfied. We had learned a lot on our 'training ship' and we had lost our gullible naiveté. I fretted about the funds that had been spent to make the final payments on her, but I had to admit that she had been good for us in many ways. Not only had we gained practical experience in boat maintenance and handling, but we had also become wiser as consumers. From that period onward we practiced one of the basic rules of survival as a purchaser: "Caveat Emptor – let the buyer beware."

How does one overcome fear, that irrational emotion that is sufficiently encompassing as to erase logic and reason? Those who have lived near the water and have experienced the joys of boating from an early age cannot possibly understand why anyone would be tense or fearful in a small boat. People who have not experienced this trepidation find it difficult to understand, and often deride or ignore signs that the partner is suffering such intense apprehension.

When talking with women who are similarly afraid and uncomfortable on the water I often think back to the fear I had experienced during my introduction to boating. Because the image of cruising tends to be, "Rah, rah, isn't this great?" many women are embarrassed, and afraid to admit to their partners that they are quietly (and sometimes, not so quietly) worried. They may be anxious about the wind, the seas, rocks, marine traffic, becoming seasick and a host of other things, regardless of how large and seaworthy their vessel may be. They get little consolation from a partner who is obviously enjoying the experience, shows few signs of concern and all too often makes comments such as, "Don't be silly, there's nothing to worry about."

This stress can so easily be mollified if the situation is talked about openly. By discussing concerns, exchanging ideas, and knowing how the other person feels, a worried partner can gain reassurance and confidence.

Knowledge and experience will of course boost one's confidence. Learning basic boat handling and maintenance, along with some navigation and emergency preparedness will assist a newcomer to feel more at home on the water and find real pleasure in active participation.

SOME DREAMS OF TRAVEL CAME TRUE

An elephant ride in the forest near Chiang Mai, Thailand

Hill Tribe kindergarten class, northern Thailand

Phra Nang beach, Thailand

Hill Tribe girl in the Golden Triangle, Thailand

The endangered yellow-eyed penguin in New Zealand

Milford Sound, South Island, New Zealand

The waterfront at Isomeer, Holland

Keukenhof Gardens, Lisse, Holland

Walls surrounding Pena Palace, Sintra, Portugal

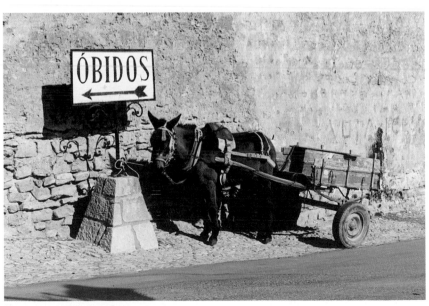

Patience in Portugal

Hardanger, Norway

Countryside near Heidelberg, Germany

Gieranger Fiord, Norway

Burg Katz above the town of St. Goarshausen on the Rhine River, Germany

Water seller at a Berber market, Morocco

Berber market between Marrakesh and Casablanca, Morocco

3   BLUE SKYS

Oh for a solid, well-built boat designed by a professional marine architect and constructed by a reputable builder! We thought we knew what we were looking for as we prowled around various marinas and boatyards in the greater Vancouver area, and in 1961 we finally came across *Blue Skys*, a 36-foot centerboard Crocker ketch constructed by a local boat builder known for his solid workmanship. Since he was already involved with the construction of his next boat he had neglected this one and she was in dire need of cosmetic attention. The price was right and she seemed to be just what we wanted. Planked with sturdy yellow cedar over oak ribs, she was a worthy candidate for an offshore voyage. To eliminate the heavy weight of the solid wooden masts we replaced the standing rigging with aluminum spars and bought new running rigging and sails for the altered rig. In addition, we replaced the makeshift steering arrangement with a commercially built steering quadrant installed by a professional shipyard.

Among boaters it is considered to be bad luck to change a vessel's name, but we had no choice, since we could not continue with the incorrect spelling painted on her stern and bows. I was a teacher, after all! When planning an offshore voyage there are certain advantages to being registered in the Lloyds Book of Registry, so we looked for a unique name, one that was related to the sea as well as having a Canadian connection. We searched through various books on the North and finally came up with *Kakoodlak,* an Inuit word that means "Bird of the Storm." Unfortunately, the "storm" part turned out to be rather prophetic, but the name did pique fellow boaters' curiosity and initiate some animated conversations and amusing situations.

One night when we were living aboard we had put out the lights and heard a fisherman mumbling as he staggered home from a night at the pub. Pausing as he came alongside our boat, he tried to pronounce the name for several minutes, going from "Kookdak," to "Kakadak" to "Koolalak" to several other slurred versions. Down below we laughed uncontrollably at his efforts as he shambled away mumbling, "Awe, t'ell with it."

Cosmetic work needed

Charles finished his degree at university and we moved onto the boat so that we could more easily turn to the many jobs that needed to be done prior to our planned departure. In the early 1960s this was considered bizarre behavior, for no one in Vancouver lived on a boat over the winter unless they were desperate. I continued to teach school, and my fellow staff members were incredulous upon learning that not only had we moved from residence at university but we were living in the lowly-sounding location of Annacis Slough. Certainly the name did not denote a classy neighborhood, and it was in fact in an undeveloped semi-industrial area off one of the channels of the Fraser River. The facility was patronized mainly by fishermen, and owned by a retired fisherman, Tom Johnson and his wife, Hanna. Tom and Hanna treated us like family and we became life-long friends. Often as we headed up the dock on a non-working day we'd hear a cheery voice calling, "Come on in for some coffee," and Hanna would bring out a big jar of freshly baked cookies to serve along with steaming cups of coffee.

One brisk winter morning as we were having breakfast we heard the faint melodic sound of fragile crystal bells. We opened the hatch to discover the source of the gentle tinkling music and saw before us an unbelievably beautiful scene. The leafless poplars bordering the slough were dressed in white hoar-frost, sparkling in the weak winter sun, while drifting down the river tiny pieces of thin ice tinkled as they jostled each other in the gently moving current. It was an unforgettable fairytale scene, one that we remembered with wonder long after.

Hoar-frost

Charles and I had always had dogs when we were growing up and we missed the joys a pet provides. We wanted to have a dog join us in our travels and felt it would be easier if it was raised on the boat from

43

an early age, rather than be introduced as an adult dog to all the challenges of sailing. We decided to buy a Springer Spaniel, a breed known to be comfortable around water. We fell in love with the first one we saw, adopted him and named him "Beau." He turned out to be a faithful friend, an excellent traveler and a happy boat dog; he was a part of our family for 13 years.

When we were under way Beau learned to wedge himself into a corner so when the boat heeled he would slide within his loose skin in only one direction. This habit was so ingrained that he always slept tucked into a corner even when we lived ashore. Since his first home was a boat tied to a dock, he was always in high spirits when we visited a marina and would run along ahead of us looking for "his boat."

Beau

When Beau was about six months old we decided to take a break from working on the boat and sail to the Gulf Islands for the long weekend. A fair wind was blowing and our new rig and sails carried us across the Strait of Georgia faster than we had anticipated. We had decided to enter the island chain through Porlier Pass, which we had not transited previously, but we made such good headway that our quick passage brought us to the pass about two hours before slack water, when the rising tide was running strong. Charles felt we had sufficient power to buck the current so he decided to attempt the passage. Once into the tidal stream our forward motion decreased quickly, until we were barely making any forward progress. As *Kakoodlak's* passage over the ground diminished in the swirling waters and strong currents Charles steadily increased the speed to maintain forward motion. The eddies became small, deep whirlpools, and at one point we were spun 90 degrees in one direction and immediately 180 degrees in the other direction in but a few seconds. It was becoming a wild ride but we carried on.

We continued to be tossed about like a toothpick. Some of our loosely stowed gear clattered to the cabin floor. Smoky, acrid fumes began to pour out of the cabin. Our first thought was of fire. Charles remained at the controls while I flew below, grabbed the fire extinguisher and peered through the smoke into the engine compartment. Smoky fumes were rising from a gap in the exhaust pipe insulation I had recently painted, but there were no flames. Foolishly, I had not used heat resistant paint and my work of art was protesting; although the fumes were harmless they gave the impression that the boat was about to erupt in flames at any moment. And then, Beau became seasick and vomited his lunch into the cockpit. What a mess!

Adding insult to injury, several people near the lighthouse on the point were lined up gazing at us with binoculars as we made our slow but action-packed and smoky way through the pass. What a relief to finally reach quiet waters beyond the maelstrom and proceed to the peaceful anchorage, aptly named Retreat Cove. With greater respect for tidal currents and the need to pay more attention to "Directions for use" on paint cans, we had learned still more lessons in the school of experience.

45

As my confidence in Charles and the boat grew I began to feel at ease in stronger winds and enjoy the exhilaration of sailing. I particularly enjoyed arriving at new anchorages, rowing the dinghy along the shoreline, going for hikes ashore and examining the wealth of marine life in tidal pools. Nevertheless, time spent sailing was still not a time of pure enjoyment, but rather something that had to be done in order to reach a destination. I was a fuss-budget and nagged about my worries. Charles quietly reminded me, "On any boat there can be only one captain. If you want to be captain, go ahead and make the decisions; otherwise I'll be captain. When I say something, do it! I'll take the responsibility for the decision and if it's wrong we can talk about it later, but don't argue about it at the time." I had no wish to be captain. Our little chat encouraged me to be a more responsive crew and one that at least hesitated before coming up with suggestions or queries.

Kakoodlak at anchor in Prideau Haven

46

4 The Dream is Blown Away

After more coastal cruises in varying weather conditions, we felt at last that we were ready to plan our long-awaited offshore voyage. There was much to be done in the year leading up to our departure, for we had planned a 4- or 5-year circumnavigation. After careful study of Pilot Charts, Sailing Directions and various references we decided that August was the best month for travel along the Washington and Oregon coast before harbor-hopping in California. Our departure was set for early August of 1963. Several hundred charts were neatly stowed in the chart table, leeboards were installed and the lockers were crammed with cameras, film, fishing gear, clothes for every climate and food for several months. Since we both had been working and saving for a year, we had managed to accumulate sufficient funds for several years of cruising.

It is impossible to describe the anticipation and anxiety that builds as you approach the first offshore voyage. Sleep comes with great difficulty, and the butterflies in your stomach keep reminding you of the momentous step that you are about to take. How exciting to be able to set off on a dream come true! There is always a certain amount of eagerness and anticipation to any cruise, but nothing matches the high level of excitement and trepidation experienced as the date approaches for your departure.

As for my fears, my longing to travel offshore overwhelmed any trepidation I may have felt, even the realization that if anything should happen to Charles I was incapable of handling many aspects of travel alone. My powerful desire for adventure overshadowed both my fears and my ignorance.

Departure from Annacis Slough

The weather gods smiled on us as we set off in high spirits from our friendly marina, through the Gulf Islands, and beyond Victoria to Neah Bay in the northwestern tip of the Olympic Peninsula in Washington. We rounded Cape Flattery in fog and from that point on lost sight of land. It was reassuring to be well off the coast, for now local boat traffic and coastal dangers were no longer a problem. The ocean had a beauty of its own, even though the gray seas seemed to melt into the distant horizon and become one with the sky.

We had two days of overcast skies, and 15-knot winds provided comfortable sailing, just what we needed while settling in to the routine of three-hour watches. Following the rhumb line, our course increasingly took us offshore, until we were over 60 miles off Cape

Mendocino. Then the barometer dropped quickly, accompanied by a rapid increase in the northwesterly swell. Heavy weather was on its way! Within a short time the seas were building and the wind rising, and glowering clouds descended and raced across the sky. We were in for a blow such as we had never seen during our coastal cruises. I was nervous, but I had confidence that the boat would see us through and that Charles had everything under control.

As the wind increased and the sea conditions deteriorated, we reduced sail again and again, until finally we were running under bare poles. To my dismay, Charles became violently seasick. We had a large variety of remedies aboard; we had expected that I would be the one to become ill, since I often felt out of sorts even in a gentle swell. However, it was Charles. He became intensely ill, and none of the remedies we had brought gave him any relief. Surprisingly, Beau and I were neither queasy nor did we lose our appetite; in fact the stress of the moment seemed to be somewhat relieved by eating! Fortunately the blow lasted for only 24 hours, after which we motor-sailed in a sloppy sea until we could set sail in moderate winds, and Charles recovered.

As it turned out, that one-day gale was just an introduction to what the Pacific Ocean would deal us. Soon after we found ourselves in a three-day storm that threatened to blow us past our destination of San Francisco. In order to reduce our speed, we rigged a sea anchor and lashed the wheel. The sound of the wind in the rigging changed its pitch from soprano to a scream, and the breaking seas became streaked and angry. The waves took turns slapping the side of the boat or resounding on the hull like sledgehammers. Beau sensed our concern and looked up with a start as the sounds vibrated throughout the boat. He cuddled up to me on the bunk, and his warmth helped to alleviate my fears. Charles again became dreadfully seasick, and soon had nothing left to vomit, his system giving way to dry heaves. He became extremely weak, and I became frightened at seeing his health deteriorate so dramatically. Here was my Captain becoming pale, weak and listless.

To add to our concern, ever since our departure from Victoria clouds had obscured the sun, preventing Charles from taking any sun shots to determine our position. As a result we tracked our progress by use of the radio direction finder, homing in on radio beacons and monitoring the change in location of local broadcast stations as we moved along the coast.

A new sound, an ominous metallic clanking from the stern, gave us our greatest worry. We waited for a series of seas that were not breaking, then we carefully opened the stern hatch to find the problem. It was a shocking development; the steering mechanism appeared to be disintegrating. The professionally-installed steering system was beginning to move from side to side as the boat rolled in the seas, producing the clunking sound we had heard. Instead of being secured by a proper bolt, a critical connection was held in place by a 5/8" brass setscrew, which now had stripped threads and had bent under the load. Our supply of spare parts had ½" but no 5/8" bolts. Desperately, we used the available supply to jury-rig the system, which would solve the problem for only a few hours at a time, to be repeated each time the clunk-clunk-clunk informed us it had given way yet again.

Rising seas

Another sound was soon added to the cacophony of wind, the periodic harsh slam of a sea against the hull, and the whoosh of water streaming along the deck. A dull, regular thump accompanied by a vibration seemed to jar the boat. We were growing increasingly worried since we couldn't find the sound's source inside the hull, but we were somewhat reassured that the boat was not taking on extra water. Later we found the cause of this problem: the rolling of the boat had caused the rudder to work from side to side causing the hole to enlarge in the bracket at its base. It was easily repaired in San Francisco, but in the midst of this storm, it was yet another concern added to the onslaught of anxieties we were undergoing at the time, including my fear and shock at Charles' continued deterioration. At any rate, sleep was fitful at best during the three days of stormy conditions. I prayed as I had never prayed before.

"Please God, stop the wind. Well if you're not going to stop it, can you just let it calm down a little?"

"I promise not to cheat on my income tax if you'll just drop the wind to 30 knots, better still, make it 20 please."

"I'll be a better person and give more money to charity. I'll . . . Just please, stop the damned wind."

The wind shrieked in response, mocking my whimpered prayers.

After becoming exhausted and completely disheartened I took two sleeping pills and collapsed into my bunk with the resigned thought: "If I wake up alive tomorrow morning then that will be satisfactory and I'll be somewhat rested; but if I wake up dead, well at least it's over with."

Feeling groggy and out of sorts, I did awake to the realization that although the boat was rocking and rolling, its motion had eased somewhat, and the scream of the wind in the rigging had been replaced by the slapping of halyards on the masts. I brewed some coffee and went up on deck to see that conditions were indeed vastly improved.

As we finished breakfast, a freighter came within hailing distance and we made contact, asking the crew to inform the Coast Guard of our position, in case we were unable to make port. The message was misunderstood by the crew, whose English was broken at best, and within a few hours a Coast Guard cutter from San Francisco appeared to offer assistance. By this time we were only a few miles from Golden Gate but we accepted their offer of a tow, for we had no more spare bolts to hold the steering quadrant together. Exhausted and saddened, we were ignominiously towed into San Francisco with only one wish: to get our feet on dry land.

We were completely demoralized. For the four years since we had bought our first boat, all our dreams had been focused on this voyage of a lifetime. Now here we were, only 700 miles from home and shamefully limping into port, ready to call it quits. For one week we tidied up the boat, hauled it to repair the steering and rudder problems, and recovered from the exhausting ordeal. We spent much of the time examining our feelings about whether or not we truly were prepared to continue with our cruising dreams.

After seeing the detrimental effects of prolonged seasickness on Charles, I felt that it was senseless for us to proceed further. He, too, was shocked at how quickly he had become seriously weakened by a seasickness for which there seemed no cure. (It was several years later that "the patch" was developed, which turned out to be the only remedy that really worked for him.) The level of his disappointment is clearly evident in his log entry, "Margo is the best man on this boat for the work she has done." It was a thoroughly heart-wrenching decision to make, but we finally came to the conclusion that our cruising dream had ended. We listed our beautiful *Kakoodlak* for sale and abandoned all our hopes and dreams we had wrapped up in her.

Kakoodlak sold in less than a month. In her place we bought a Corvair Monza coupe (made infamous by Ralph Nader), rented a U-Haul, and turned our backs on the ocean to head for a two-month exploration of the spectacular National Parks and Monuments of Southern California, Arizona and New Mexico. The beauty of the deserts and mountains and the overall charm of the American southwest were a balm to our shattered feelings. Though I secretly harbored second thoughts about whether our decision had been hasty, logic told me that it was a dream that was not to be. The Rubicon had been crossed; we would move on.

Bryce Canyon, Utah

Our next plan was to return to Vancouver and consider living an "ordinary" life.

"Can't we do something normal for a change and buy a house and just be like regular people? I queried.

"That sounds like a possible idea."

"We can go back to hiking in the mountains with maybe some easy climbing—no first ascents, just comfortable scrambling."

"Well, Beau will be happier. He won't have to stagger to the foredeck in sloppy seas just to answer the call of nature."

So it was agreed that we would forget sailing, keep our feet on the ground and "try to be normal." This down-to-earth plan lasted until we approached the Columbia River Valley, where we rounded a corner and had a glimpse of the wide river and a small powerboat zooming over the water. Almost in unison we both burst out "Oh, doesn't that look like fun?" Then we started to laugh as we both added, "But it's a power boat—just think how much nicer it would be if it were a sailboat."

From that moment on we knew that we were to be forever bitten by the sailing bug, and that our cruising days had been only briefly interrupted.

Back to the mountains

54

What went wrong on this venture? Now that years have passed I feel confident to provide an answer. To begin with, we had bad luck in meeting two bouts of heavy weather in our first offshore trip, even though it was one of the best months to transit this part of the coast. Then, the heavy weather caused Charles' intense seasickness, for which there were no available remedies at the time. And finally, the near loss of steering ability was a direct result of poor workmanship by a "professional" yard.

What should we have done differently? Firstly, we should have been more thorough in checking that the steering mechanism was properly installed and could stand up to rigorous conditions. We relied entirely on specialists to do a professional job, but should have checked that it could stand up to heavy loads placed on it. Secondly, since our coastal cruising in relatively benign British Columbia waters had not tested our reaction to heavy seas, it would have been wise to have crewed on a boat making a similar trip, to get first-hand experience in ocean travel. I believe that part of Charles' seasickness was a result of extreme worry and tension during storms, compounded by the motion of the boat. Later, of course, medication was developed that prevented his problem. Hindsight, practical experience and medical advances make solutions so simple!

5   *Windigo*

Upon our return to Vancouver, we bought a house and attempted to live as landlubbers. Charles resumed work with an engineering firm, but spent his spare time designing a 34-foot cruising cutter. Then, three months later we were transferred to Toronto where he was seconded to work for Atomic Energy of Canada for a two-year period. We had been happy living in Vancouver where our outdoor interests could find involvement in activities in nearby mountains and the sea, so we were reluctant to accept this posting. However, we felt that it would provide an opportunity to experience life in central Canada and to visit the Maritimes. Also, as a reward for agreeing to leave the west for two years his employer had agreed to give us a six-month leave of absence at the end of our eastern sojourn. We quickly developed a new set of travel plans, a trip down the intra-coastal waterway to Florida and the Bahamas. With these dreams in mind we packed our gear and set out on the road to Toronto, with Beau happily sleeping in the back seat of the car.

Our newest plan was to have the boat Charles had designed built in the Maritimes, where shipwrights have been famous for over a century as the best wooden boat builders on the continent. We sent Charles' boat plans to a number of recommended boat builders in Nova Scotia and New Brunswick and asked for a quotation on construction costs. Then, for our vacation at the end of the first year, we drove to the different yards to have a first-hand look at the quality of the workmanship and to decide which would be contracted to build our next boat.

However, this turned out to be a sad trip, for we were witnessing the end of an era in Maritime history. Several of the yards were no longer in production, while others were operated by elderly men whose sons weren't interested in carrying on the business; they wanted 9 to 5 jobs with paid holidays and specified fringe benefits. John Barkhouse of Chester, Nova Scotia was building a 50-foot mahogany sloop for a New York lawyer. I rubbed my hands over the smooth hull and commented to Charles,

"Just feel this, it's like satin."

I was quickly rebuffed by Mr. Barkhouse who snapped in a gravelly voice,

"What do you mean? It's rough, it's only had its third sanding!"

Mr. Barkhouse liked Charles' blueprints, but he felt that he just didn't have the health and energy to build another boat. He gazed sadly at the boat he was building and said, "No, I'm sorry but this is the last boat I'll ever build."

Pinaud's yacht basin, Baddeck, Nova Scotia

Some of the other builders did submit quotes, but the quality of their work was not up to that of Mr. Barkhouse. Only the Pinaud yard in beautiful Bras d'or Lakes showed workmanship of similar quality, but their quotation of $17,000 was a lot of money in 1965—money that we didn't have.

Disappointed but not deterred, we returned to Toronto, and Charles suggested that we look into buying a catamaran, as its shoal draft would be ideal for cruising the shallow waters of the Bahamas. We looked at vessels being built at several yards, with construction consisting of ¼" plywood covered with a thin layer of fiberglass. However, I simply couldn't bring myself to feel safe with the idea of such a flimsy hull separating us from the bottom of the ocean.

"I just cannot feel secure if I can't have a sturdy boat taking us offshore. We'll have to look for something else."

As a last resort I suggested cheerfully, "Let's look into buying a used boat."

Charles' response was quick and terse, "We've already looked at boats in marinas and boatyards throughout Ontario. There wasn't one that could interest us; most of them are day sailors for inland lakes, or they are racing machines."

Undeterred by his comment, and determined to check out this avenue of approach, I turned to the yellow pages and phoned the first yacht broker in the Directory, describing the kind of vessel we were looking for. He listened quietly and readily replied,

"I think I have just the boat for you—the dimensions are perfect and she is a sound, seaworthy vessel built by John Barkhouse."

I drew a quick breath and triumphantly repeated to be sure I had heard correctly,

"You said the builder was Barkhouse and she's a 34-foot mahogany cutter?" Charles heard, and his face lit up....now he was interested!

The next weekend we drove to Sarnia, Ontario, where *Windigo* was on the hard, as all vessels are hauled during the winter months to escape the ice of Lake Huron. Though she was covered with tarps to protect her from the harsh winter weather, we could see John Barkhouse' quality workmanship written all over her. It was eerie—the dimensions of the boat Charles had designed were 34'9" with a 10' beam and the vessel we were looking at was 34'6" with a 9'6" beam. A bid from another interested buyer was to be presented within a week, so we had to act quickly. Instead of an even amount we added an extra hundred dollars and it made the difference. Our offer was accepted; *Windigo* was ours!

We waited impatiently for the ice to melt on Lake Huron and the boats to be dropped in the water. I do mean "dropped," for the method used was one we'd not seen previously. A crane on a caterpillar tractor would lift each boat from its cradle, transport it to the water's edge and then slowly lower it over the water. At some point in the process the land side treads would be lifted clear off the ground by the weight of the boat as it descended. When the boat was released the tractor dropped back into its normal position with both treads on terra firma. We watched tensely when *Windigo*'s turn came and she was smoothly returned to her element.

Launching Windigo in Sarnia, Ontario
59

We returned to Toronto for a week or two, and then during the long Easter weekend we boarded the train for Sarnia to prepare *Windigo* for the trip through Detroit and beyond to her temporary new home in Lake Ontario. I was somewhat concerned about the trip across shallow 250-mile long Lake Erie, which has an unenviable reputation for building sharp, short seas when the prevailing winds pick up. Prior to departing I stopped in at a local coffee shop, and a couple of elderly men resembling characters from a Mark Twain novel started to chat with me.

"Are you the new owners of *Windigo* and takin' her to the bright lights of Trona?"

"Yes, it's our first time sailing on the Great Lakes."

"Well," the man with a crumpled hat and heavy mackintosh jacket responded with a raspy voice, "There's one spot you'd best be careful of."

My ears perked up, for here was local knowledge that could be important.

"What spot is that?" I queried.

"Oh," he croaked, "I reckon it's Lake Erie you better be careful of."

"Thanks a lot," I smiled weakly and left, wondering if once more we were going to be in for trouble.

With no wind, we motored south in the Lake St. Clare River past Detroit and entered the western end of Lake Erie. There we found ourselves in a marked channel facing a cool, brisk headwind, with sharp seas that caused our lightly laden boat to pound. I heated up a can of chicken noodle soup to give us a hot and easily prepared bite to eat. A few minutes later Charles went down below to get his foul weather gear and he returned with the dishpan with clearly identifiable noodles swimming around in the bottom.

"What are you doing with more soup?" I asked.

"Noodle soup is just as good coming up as it is going down," he replied. Good grief, he was seasick again and the trip had barely started!

In spite of our concerns, the trip across Lake Erie turned out to be one long motoring day after another, with just enough tail winds to bring the exhaust fumes into the cockpit. With limited time to make the trip we motored on and on until we reached the eastern end of Lake Erie and moored at the upper end of the Welland Canal. This was to be our first experience transiting a canal and we were about to descend 325 feet in the 27-mile long waterway. The descent of the eight locks of the Welland Ship Canal was uneventful, for the water just drained out of each lock like water from a bathtub with only a few weak currents swirling about.

Typical Lake Erie fishing boat

It was a remarkable experience to travel the length of one of Canada's greatest engineering projects. The first canal to join Lake Erie to Lake Ontario was completed in 1829 by a private company. Subsequently it was taken over, first by Upper Canada and then by the

Federal government, which has undertaken many improvements, even including reforestation to protect vessels from crosswinds. Used by the largest bulk carriers on the Great Lakes, it is an important part of the Saint Lawrence Seaway.

After exiting from Port Weller, we sailed to Port Dalhousie and moored for the night. The next day found us crossing to the north side of Lake Ontario to Marie Curtis Park. This was to be our live-aboard home for a few months, since it is located between Toronto and Oakville, convenient to Charles' place of work. The narrow inlet had space for less than 20 boats and our spot was a snug fit for *Windigo*.

One evening after dinner we heard some shouting and the engine of a nearby vessel being revved up erratically. We climbed to the cockpit to see what the commotion was about, and to our astonishment were faced with a powerboat bearing down on our stern with the motor roaring. I jumped into the cockpit and Charles yelled at me,

"Don't try to fend it off, you'll get hurt."

Just then the drunken boater, unable to control his vessel, rammed our stern with a thump, and a loud cracking sound was heard. We rushed to the stern and looked in dismay at the damage—the large, lovely piece of 2" Honduras mahogany that made up the transom was shattered and cracked at deck level. Although the offender's insurance covered the cost of repairs, it was impossible to find a replacement piece for the entire transom, and the obviously patched section was a constant reminder of this needless damage.

In September of 1965, our two-year sojourn in Ontario ended and we were ready to set off again. It was with great pride that we hoisted the distinctive red maple leaf of Canada's new flag, even though we subsequently had to explain to boaters in the United States that it wasn't to be confused with that of the USSR. The novelty of having our own distinctive flag brought back memories of an art assignment to design a Canadian emblem, done many years in the past in the one-room country school I had attended as a youngster.

Beau on guard

Once again, since we wanted to document the boat, it was necessary to rename her unless we wanted to call her *Windigo V* following the four *Windigos* already listed in *Lloyd's Register of Shipping*. Though we liked the name that meant 'the spirit of the wind in the trees,' we wanted a name that had not already been registered. Our experience with *Kakoodlak's* difficult pronunciation and length (which caused extra work when removing letters during spring brush-up) prompted us to look for something different: a marine bird with a short name that was easy to pronounce. To our delight, the name *Ern* filled our requirements and had not already been registered. The only problem with this appellation was that when giving the name we would be met with quizzical looks and inquiries: "*Urn*??" as if to say "Do you have a death wish or something?" However, crossword aficionados recognize the name for what it is, an east coast sea eagle. It suited us just fine!

6   East Coast Adventure

We were excited and keen to begin a new journey. Charts, provisions, engine spares and tools were assembled and that old thrill of setting off in new waters once again lit up our beings. As we prepared for our trip through the Erie Canal with its numerous low bridges, it was necessary to pull the mast and mount it on deck, which was accomplished by installing a series of wooden braces that supported it securely. In addition, it was tied with a network of lines that made the boat resemble a game of Cat's Cradle. While the altered placement of weight seemed to make *Ern* rather tender, the main change was the difficulty of moving back and forth on the deck to handle the bow and stern line or fend off when mooring to a dock. Fortunately, I was in good shape so weaving my way through the network of lines and supports was accomplished fairly smoothly. As for Beau, he was just happy to be on a boat again and have our constant companionship. All of us looked forward to our new adventure with enthusiastic good spirits.

Herb, a steelworker friend from Hamilton, asked if he could join us for the trip up the Welland Canal as he thought it "might prove interesting." We gladly took him aboard to help with manning the lines, reducing the need for movement on deck, which was awkward at best. The southbound passage up the Canal was a stark contrast to the uneventful day we had taken to descend from Lake Erie to Lake Ontario, for we were locked through with *Pinedale*, a typical lake

freighter over 600 feet long. Dwarfed by its huge bulk, we were like a
toy compared with this robust behemoth. Each time we entered one of
the eight locks, two light lines were lowered from above, to each of
which we attached a long line with a large eye spliced in the end. These
were hoisted up and looped around a bollard, and we took in the slack
as the water level in the lock was raised.

Our lock partner Pinedale

Pinedale gave us a fright as she followed us into each lock, her
black, blunt bows coming closer and closer as she inched forward to
take her place. When her wire hawsers tightened and brought her
forward motion to a halt, they protested with disconcerting screeches
and groans, and we watched in fear and trepidation as the monstrous
shape was slowly reined in. We felt as if *Ern* was a trapped rat boxed
into a corner of rough cement walls as *Pinedale* lumbered forward to
within less than 40 feet of our relatively tiny, fragile vessel.

Then as each lock filled, water gushed into the confined space,
creating wild turbulence and forcing us to fend the boat off the sides of
the lock while we took in the lines. With no support from the long lines

reaching high overhead we felt like a marionette in a maelstrom, and we had to keep the motor running at all times to help control the boat. *Ern* rolled sharply as her long straight keel felt the full force of the boiling water. We had expected confused water as each lock filled, but this was chaotic. Since each lock had its own peculiarities as to amount and character of the turbulence, we never quite knew just what to expect.

There was a short distance to travel between the first three locks that gave us time to catch our breath and enjoy a snack as we glided through the green, pleasant landscape of southern Ontario. Only a few trees had changed to their fall colors, so that the scene beyond the roadway was mainly a monochrome painting in shades of green. The view of the peaceful countryside provided a calming alternative to the outbursts of adrenalin we expended at each lock. Arduous as it was, we were thankful to be making a memorable passage on a special waterway rather than coping with the hectic pace of highway traffic. A top speed of 6 knots was quite satisfactory, for we were on vacation and an exploration of new waters lay ahead.

Turbulence in the Welland Canal

Since Locks 4, 5, and 6, were grouped together, we were barely clear of one before entering the next. The last of the trio was downright dangerous, for the turbulence was so bad that even the use of the motor and Herb's strong arms manning the ropes couldn't prevent several hard bumps on the lock walls. Before leaving we had prepared sturdy fenders for this part of the trip: four two-by-fours covered on three sides with carpet now hung over the sides of the hull. Commercial yacht fenders would have been crushed and destroyed by those menacing knobby walls that were streaked with oil, tar and scum. At any rate, our homemade fenders may not have looked pretty but they survived the passage and were used successfully throughout the Erie Canal.

Motoring on a long stretch toward the last three locks was a different kind of excitement, for *Pinedale* continued to make us uneasy as she came ever closer to our stern. We soon realized that she wanted to make better time than the top speed we were capable of, and so she was following us in such a way that her bulging bow wave lifted us up. In fact, we were surfing on it, and thus both vessels were able to make better time. Even so, because of a four-hour delay at one of the locks, it took 12 tiring hours to transit the Canal. It was dark when we exited the last lock and traveled to a nearby marina, too tired to celebrate our first major step.

"Well Herb, did this day turn out to be as interesting as you had hoped?"

"Believe me, there were quite a few times when I was glad it was your boat and not mine," he replied with feeling.

"I had no idea this day would be so exhausting. Thank goodness you were here to help with the big push when it was needed.

We agreed that it had been a taxing job to complete this marathon. After mooring *Ern,* Herb left us to return to Hamilton, and Charles and I collapsed into our bunks, glad to know we had passed a major hurdle without damage to the boat. *Ern* was safe so far!

Upon reaching Buffalo we cleared Customs to enter the United States and proceeded down the Niagara River. It was quite exciting to feel the current as we motored within less than 5 miles above Niagara Falls. The Universal Utility 4 gasoline engine had been reliable up to this point, but I still constantly eyed the shoreline, thinking that if the engine stopped we'd have to anchor in a hurry or else deliberately run aground. It was with considerable relief that we made the sharp turn to enter the approach to the western end of the Erie Canal at Tonawanda, New York. After traveling a short distance, we arrived at Lockport, where we obtained the Lock Permit allowing us to transit still more locks, thirty-five of them, that separated us from the Hudson River at Troy and Albany.

Reading Walter D. Edmonds classic novel *Erie Water* while traveling the canal brought to life for us the time when the canal was built. Completed in 1825, the Erie Canal joined the Great Lakes with the Atlantic Ocean, and was instrumental in opening up the West, allowing raw materials to reach markets in the East. In addition, it helped New York City to become the financial center of the country, for tolls charged from 1825 until 1882 earned the state of New York many times what it had cost to build the Canal. Travel was painfully slow in those days, with horses and mules hauling the barges along. An interesting reminder of how much communication has changed since the early 1800s is that in order to send news of the opening of the Canal from Buffalo to Sandy Hook, 500 miles away, a series of cannon on the route were fired, each one a signal to the next in line. It took eighty-one minutes from the time the first cannon was fired for the message to reach its destination!

Our first day on the Canal was idyllic. The sun was shining from a sky dotted with fluffy cumulus clouds, and the shirt-sleeve weather found us motoring past neatly tended gardens and lawns of attractive homes lining the Canal. Several people enjoying the fine weather waved and wished us a great trip. What a wonderful send-off; our hearts were full.

Passing under the low bridges of the Canal took some getting used to, compared to the lofty structures we were used to such as Vancouver's Lion's Gate Bridge and the Golden Gate in San Francisco. My diary expresses concern, "The bridge looks quite low. I think it'll be rather close—I'd like to slow down but Charles said 'No.' He took the tiller and we made it! I won't fuss when we come to the next one, but I reserve the right to duck my head."

Low bridge ahead

Travel along the Erie Canal was filled with constantly changing sights and sounds. Many of the sleepy towns looked as if time had stood still, with their old-style weathered buildings, sparse traffic and a few pedestrians meandering down the streets. Some houses facing the Canal had verandas where old people could be seen watching the passing parade of traffic: boats of all shapes and sizes, and tugs slowly chugging along with their barges and booms. Some of the more affluent homes had screened porches, indicating a lusty mosquito population that fortunately was inactive at this time of year. Between the small towns, much of the countryside was surprisingly untouched. Another reward of travel in September was the wonderfully strident fall scene that now lit up the waterway with reflections of gold, tangerine and crimson leaves contrasted with the greens of conifers.

Our approach to one of the locks was like a scene out of a Norman Rockwell painting. From a distance we could see two elderly men sitting on a bench on the port side of the lock. Clearly they were enjoying their pipes and commenting with a chuckle and periodic spit into the Canal as another pleasure boater provided entertainment. They had a ringside seat to watch the ever-changing show. At this particular lock, currents were more evident in the water than in the previous locking areas, and in order to take a line ashore it was necessary to climb up some particularly long steps indented into the slimy concrete walls. In a gingerly manner I made my way forward, but I attacked the steps with gusto, taking great care not to slip, drop the line or hesitate, as I made the last long step at the top where one would need to be a rather tall gorilla to comfortably reach a handhold. The old codgers watched in silence, with a look of interested expectation, as if they were hoping I would fall flat on my face, but determined not to give them the satisfaction of a guffaw, I fixed the lines without giving them the benefit of a glance. As we waited for the lock to close I heard Charles quietly congratulating me,

"Good show, girl, good show—they were just hoping you'd mess up so they'd have a laugh and one more story to tell about green, helpless yachtsmen."

One of the sounds we could have done without was to be awakened on several mornings by the patter of raindrops on the cabin top. Fog and rain combined with cool headwinds made travel rather uncomfortable, and we often chose to keep the cockpit cover on for long stretches between locks, with the result that our boat resembled a misplaced covered wagon. Then one morning toward the end of September frost on the deck reminded us that winter was approaching, and that we must press on regardless of the weather.

Sunrise on the Erie Canal

At the end of ten days of cool headwinds and showers, we reached the last lock at Troy and heaved a sigh of relief as we entered the Hudson River. No more locks! At Catskill the mast was stepped at a boatyard whose staff had no idea of what to do. Charles reticently coached them at every stage, and I watched the process as frayed nerves and tempers were barely kept just below the surface. At last the job was completed. What a pleasure to have the mast and the rigging in place and know that we would be free to move on deck without the spider web of ropes we had lived with for the past two weeks.

We still had to use the motor, as it was impossible to sail in the narrow channel of the Hudson River, where there was noticeably more traffic of both commercial and pleasure craft than in the slow-moving, peaceful Erie Canal. Just beyond the marked route, duck hunting blinds scattered in the shallow river gave a clear warning that the channel markers were to be followed precisely!

71

Travel down the Hudson River was like leafing through a maga-
zine about the rich and famous. The mansions owned by millionaires
such as the Astor and Roosevelt families overlooked the waterway and
were in stark contrast to the numerous small houses we had seen in
upper New York State. We didn't have a lot of money, yet we felt we
were the fortunate ones. Who cared what happened on the stock
market—we didn't have anything to lose!

With *Ern* moored in Englewood Cliffs, New Jersey, we spent a
busy day in New York City. We shopped for charts, a 30-pound anchor
and bags of gear. These we lugged on and off "A" and "D" trains,
subways and buses, while astonished New Yorkers stared at us as if we
were from another world. It was true, we were. My diary sums up my
feelings, "The subway scared me: really a person just doesn't have a
chance if anything goes wrong. And the noise! I'd rather be at sea."

Sailing our own boat through New York Harbor was a memorable experience. As we gazed at the bumper-to-bumper traffic of
hundreds of people heading off to work on the roads and freeways
lining the shore, we were reminded of leaf-cutting ants blindly following in line with their minds in neutral. How lucky we were! We were
young, we had no debts and we had five more months of cruising
ahead of us.

While a brisk northwesterly wind raised white caps across New
York Harbor, an unbelievable variety of tugs, ferries, barges, cruise
ships, freighters, water taxis and pleasure craft somehow managed to
dash back and forth without colliding in the confused waters. After
spending a month plodding along with relatively few boats in sight, we
were intimidated by the hectic pace of the congested marine traffic. To
add to the mayhem, a garbage barge hauling rubbish out to sea caught
fire, and soon fireboats were dashing across the harbor to congregate
near the flaming, smoking, smelly mess. As if the harbor bedlam wasn't
enough to occupy our minds, the wind suddenly became gusty and
blew well above the 25-knots predicted. Flying along at hull speed we

were glad to exit Verezzano Narrows and enter Ambrose Channel, where we gazed in awe at the Statue of Liberty. After an exciting day of heads-up maneuvering to avoid collision with the heavy traffic, it was a relief to at last leave behind the chaos of New York Harbor.

New York Harbor

Following a stopover in Atlantic City we proceeded to Cape May, where the day ended with a dramatic and scary night entrance. We had wasted several hours entering Great Egg Inlet with the hopes of traveling to Ocean City. Now, Charles realized too late that there was a fixed bridge with 35-foot clearance, and we were forced to retreat and continue down the coast toward our destination. We were able to get a lift from a headsail until the wind turned southeasterly and began to raise the kind of head sea *Ern* doesn't like. The waves were the right configuration for her to hobbyhorse, and they slowed her speed as her bow ploughed into each trough, making the motion very uncomfortable. I climbed into the forward bunk, foolishly hoping that some extra weight in the forward part of the boat would help to alleviate her thrashing motion. I was almost lifted off the bunk as the bow bounced

73

up and down with rhythmic crashes. I started to feel queasy, so I quietly retreated to the cockpit, wishing that *Ern* had a more powerful engine.

The evening turned into night as we continued our tortuous passage down the coast. I was becoming apprehensive. I both dreaded and yearned for arrival at the harbor entrance, for much as I wanted to arrive at our destination, I disliked making a night entrance in rough seas into a strange harbor, particularly one with a narrow, rock-lined channel. It was very tempting to chide Charles for not reading the critical information sooner but, knowing it wouldn't change the situation, I kept my peace.

I went below to make a cup of coffee, feeling foolishly reassured that everything would be all right as I lit the kerosene lamps and their warm glow filled the cabin. Beau welcomed me with a friendly bunt and I tried to be cheerful as I said, "Just a few more minutes of this miserable trip, old boy. Cheer up and as soon as we get to port we'll go for a walk." He heard the magic words and optimistically wagged his tail and smiled as only a Springer Spaniel can do. Quite irrationally, the combination of the sheltered cabin and Beau's positive response gave a lift to my spirits. I returned to the cockpit, we quickly downed the coffee and cookies, then I leaned into the cabin, put the empty mugs in the sink and closed the hatch.

By the time we reached the entrance to the channel at Cape May the seas had become breaking swells. Charles warned,

"Hang on when we turn, we'll be in the trough of the waves and it's going to be a rough ride."

"How soon will we turn the corner?"

"Not soon enough."

He shone the searchlight on the sharp, glistening boulders of the breakwater—the rocks looked dreadfully close and very solid. When we turned into the channel, *Ern* was flung violently on her side with her gunwale in the water, as I clung to the boom support for dear life. The mugs crashed to the floor and there were some other unidentifiable sounds. Charles shone the searchlight on the other side of the channel; It looked so close! I prayed, "Please, God don't let this be the end of our trip."

Ern floundered about for what seemed like an eternity but in fact was only a few seconds, until we entered the protected water within the channel. When all was quiet at last, I opened the hatch to see what the commotion had been in the cabin. As I started to open the hatch Beau's speckled nose and then his whole head squeezed through the opening. In terror he had climbed up the steep companionway, which normally would have been impossible for him on his own. He looked quite dismayed. Springer Spaniels usually have rather sagging lower eyelids, but this time they were downright drooping, as if he had a hangover. No wonder he was upset; the scene below was a mess! The library of books that once lined both sides of the shelves above our bunks was strewn on the floor of the cabin, along with the empty mugs. Poor Beau had been bombarded from all directions by the falling missiles and had endured an even more traumatic entrance to Cape May than we had. As soon as we let him into the cockpit all was forgiven as he snuggled up against us, looking for a cuddle.

The red navigation lights within the harbor were difficult to distinguish from the traffic lights and the brake lights of automobiles on shore. Tired and somewhat traumatized we groped our way within the harbor—only to run aground on a sand bank. We launched the dinghy and set the anchor to try to kedge the boat free, but to no avail. Fortunately the tide began to rise after a couple of hours and we floated free, and finally at 1:00 a.m., we tied up at a marina and collapsed into our bunks.

The following day strong headwinds were forecast, and we were thankful to stay in Cape May to shop, rest and tidy the boat, taking care also to rig extra lines to keep the library in its place. We had a great sail up Delaware Bay, then we anchored at Reedy Island rather than tackle the traffic and currents in the Delaware-Chesapeake Canal as night approached. Beau insisted on going ashore, as land was in sight, but "shore" turned out to be a soggy swamp. He took a few steps, then almost walked backwards to get into the dinghy and return to the boat. We felt sorry for him as he paced back and forth before finally doing his business on the foredeck.

People often wonder how a dog's elimination is handled at sea. Beau was hesitant about heeding the call of nature on "his boat" and he generally exercised complete control as long as land was in sight. When cruising on coastal waters we made a point of launching the dinghy and taking him ashore soon after the anchor was set. But when we were offshore it would take an hour or so of pacing before he would finally let go on the foredeck. This was the best place he could relieve himself, for it was easy to clean off the remains with a bucket of seawater. We kept reassuring him that he was a "Good Dog," but he never seemed convinced, and would always give us an apologetic glance as if to say, "Sorry, but I just couldn't help it."

During our transit of the Chesapeake and Delaware Canal the heavy marine traffic and strong currents kept us on our toes. After stopping in Chesapeake City, we tied to pilings near the shore, but this was not a good stopover for us. It started with some rough-looking teenagers coming around and asking too many questions. They spoke rudely, demanding to know who we were, where we were going and what our plans were. During the night they returned and threw rocks on the deck, waking us with a start. When I flung open the hatch and looked out they drove off, but it was impossible to sleep after that, wondering if they would return. It reminded us of the thugs who had started to come aboard in the middle of the night when we were tied to the dock in Marie Curtis Park in Lake Ontario. Fortunately, on that occasion, Beau, woken from a deep sleep on deck, sent them on their way in noisy fashion. No country has a monopoly on thugs.

Cruising down Chesapeake Bay consisted of a series of pleasant

sails, separated by some days under motor and others waiting for
strong headwinds to diminish. A highlight of this section of our trip
was meeting Anne and Eric Hiscock, whose books opened up the world
of offshore cruising to modern sailors. We had been following a
narrow, sinuous channel marked by crooked sticks at rakish angles,
leading to an anchorage in the Piankatank River when we recognized
Wanderer III. As soon as our anchor was set, sitting side by side, they
rowed over and invited us for cocktails in the evening. We readily
accepted and thoroughly enjoyed a visit in a cabin we knew so well
from the illustrations in their book, *Around the World in Wanderer III*.

When entering the bay the Hiscocks had gone aground, and had

Swinging the lead line

been pulled off by Captain Joe Jackson, a retired boater. He invited
them to see local points of interest and to bring any other boaters who
might be in the anchorage, so we were invited to join the tour. We were
happy to accept the invitation, for Charles had been a student of the
Civil War and found the prospect especially promising. We were driven
to the famous Civil War battlefields of Yorkton, Williamsburg and

Jamestown—historic yet sad reminders of the human price paid for war.

The days were getting shorter and the cold wind, often accompanied by gloomy skies and drizzle, kept reminding us that we must hurry south. When we reached Norfolk, Virginia, we found ourselves at the start of the Intra-Coastal Waterway, a series of inlets, sounds and natural waterways connected by buoyed channels. Providing a protected watercourse as far as Miami, the route is a favorite passage for east coast sailors, with some of those we met bragging that this was their umpteenth trip along the waterway. Passage within sight of the immense facilities of the U.S. Navy and miles of mothballed relics from the Second World War was an eye-opener. Rank upon rank of huge vessels, lined the shore many of them relegated to nothing more than floating granaries for excess stores, though it was good to see them being used for peaceful purposes.

Inland waterway marker with comorants

One of the highlights of the northern part of the waterway was meeting the crew of another southbound vessel, *Kahlua*, and anchoring with them in a channel near Bogue Inlet. Huge sand dunes could be seen beyond the scrub and grassy shores, and the sound of the Atlantic surf beyond beckoned us to go for a hike after dinner. A brilliant, full moon lit the white dunes, and the five of us hiked for about half a mile before reaching the beach, where the pounding surf was breaking heavily. The crests of breakers were visible well offshore as they reflected the moon's bright rays, while the phosphorescence shone from within as they crashed on the hard sand beach with a thunderous roar. They mesmerized us for over an hour, until someone noticed that it was past midnight and reminded us that we had a long day ahead of us. In addition to a few shells I picked a large handful of dry, tall sea oats from the tufts scattered on the dunes, which have been part of a dried flower arrangement ever since!

We returned to the boats to find that the strong tidal currents had now reversed direction, causing both anchors to drag, with *Kahlua* hard aground. It took an hour to tow them off and re-set bow and stern anchors in the strong currents after which we had no difficulty falling asleep, for it had been both a memorable day and an exhausting evening.

We caught up with a single-handed vessel whose skipper had a reputation for being constantly drunk, attempting night entrances and regularly going aground. Marina operators frequently asked if we had seen him, and boats were often sent to give assistance. We heard him singing before we rounded a corner and saw him off the marked channel. When he focused on us he called out,

"Ah, ah, ken you give me a tow? I'm stuck in the mud."

"We've got a deeper draft than you so we can't come very close."

"Oh dammit, be good guys and pull me off."

We heaved a monkey fist to him, but each time he was unable to catch it as he staggered on the foredeck. Hauling it in we cast it several times, but he was unable to grasp the line before it fell overboard. Beau's retrieving instincts came to the fore and as he leaned out to watch and maybe even retrieve the ball of the monkey fist, he fell overboard. With a look of panic on his face he was clearly aware that he was being swept away from *Ern* by the current. Swimming hard enough to rise well above the surface of the water, he came alongside. With a burst of adrenalin, Charles reached down and picked up our 65-pound, soaking wet dog with one hand and swung him aboard. Beau's worried demeanor changed to happiness as he thanked us with a nuzzle and a shake sending a shower of cold water over us. As for the distressed sailor, all we could do was to call out, "The tide is rising so you should float off in an hour or so."

After traveling in protected waters, we became careless one day and, although the morning sky was overcast, we failed to listen to the weather forecast. After passing through Lockwood's Folly Inlet we were buffeted about by gusty, erratic winds and noticed horizontal glowering clouds racing across the sky like rolled up blankets with frayed ends. Something else struck us as odd, for there was much less marine traffic in the waterway than we had been accustomed to seeing. It was only after we listened to the radio that we learned there had been a tornado warning in 14 counties in North Carolina and snow in Tennessee. Subsequently we paid more attention to weather reports, for we had been foolishly oblivious to the danger of tornados in this part of the country. Other weather patterns surprised us, for the further south we traveled the greater became our expectation of warm temperatures. It was only the first week of November, yet it was so cold that we had to turn on the heater and wear both our warmest sweaters and foul weather gear.

In the Carolinas the waterway became a narrow channel, with miles of swamps on either side. Shoaling was a constant problem and we touched a soft, muddy bottom several times even though we were in the channel. Sometimes we could anchor in a niche at the side of the channel, but the ground was seldom firm enough to take Beau for a walk ashore. It was here we saw the first palmettos and pelicans, a welcome sight heralding our arrival in southern waters.

Bon appetit!

One of the joys of traveling through marshy areas was the chance to fish for crabs from the boat. The method was simple and effective. Turkey necks or backs were hung over the side of the boat on a string long enough to reach the bottom, usually no more than 2 fathoms or so. A half dozen or so of these cords were hung from the life lines with their tempting morsels, waiting for a hungry crab to come along. After a half hour the string was slowly brought up until the crab was just below the surface of the water, at which point it was an easy feat to capture it with a landing net and dump it into a bucket of water. Crabs that were too small to bother with could be just raised above the surface of the water, at which time they would let go of the bait and fall back to live another day. The turkey necks could be used for several days, and when decomposition set in they became even more effective, perhaps because their strong scent traveled more quickly than that of fresh turkey. The odd whiff of rotten turkey from the after deck was a small price to pay for a quick and easy meal of fresh-caught crab!

On one occasion we had six more crabs than were needed for salad, so it was decided that we would keep them fresh in a bucket of water overnight. In the morning we noticed that one was missing. We looked in all the likely nooks and dark corners throughout the boat but were unable to locate it, so we finally gave up and popped the remaining five into a pot of boiling water. Later, when quietly sitting on the head I heard a small, scratching sound nearby. The missing crab, just barely visible, was peering up at me from behind the toilet with his spiny antennae waving back and forth! With a squeal I flew out of the head in a state of animated agitation. Charles got a lot of mileage during cruisers' tall tale sessions, describing the story of the missing crab and my unsophisticated entrance to the main cabin.

When traveling in Georgia there was a particularly long passage through miles of swamp between stopovers. Unfortunately, we slept in and our departure was delayed. We began with a tedious trip of over 60 miles, at times getting a lift from the current but at other periods having to fight an opposing flow. Eventually we realized that we wouldn't reach the hoped-for destination until well after nightfall, when travel on the waterway is ill advised because of variable currents and channel markers that are often some distance apart.

A change of plan was clearly indicated, so we approached Duplin River, in Dobury Sound, with the intention of looking for a possible anchorage. This would be well off the channel, and the chart showed some possible spots. Next to the shore that was heavily forested with palmetto, cypress and tall trees draped with grandfather's beard was a substantial dock where a large motor vessel was moored. As we passed it a slight, wiry man waved us over and invited us to tie up. We gladly accepted his kind invitation, since it would make walking Beau much easier than a shore trip by dinghy, which involved fighting strong currents and slogging through wet swamps.

We moored *Ern,* and Beau and I went for a walk on the incon-spicuous gravel road leading through the thick growth of trees. Sud-denly there opened up the most surprising scene: an avenue bordered by dark cypress and blooming camellias stretched for about a quarter of a mile in the distance. Beyond the colorful border lay an expanse of manicured lawns edged by a rich green forest. What a sight! Beau went bounding after a deer peacefully grazing on the lush grass, but when it simply looked at him without moving he ran back and hid behind me. We wandered back to the dock and there fell into conversation with Cheryl, a friendly lady who turned out to be the local teacher. Since I too, had been a teacher, we chatted easily and she asked if we would like to go for a ride around the island the following day.

As we bounded along in her old Ford pick-up we learned that we had landed on Sapelo Island, the summer home of the Reynolds family, a name well-known in the manufacture of cigarettes. The road wound through huge trees decked with Spanish moss, until arriving at a magnificent sprawling mansion. Numerous replicas of statues, such as Michaelangelo's "David," were scattered along broad walkways and bordered the huge indoor and outdoor swimming pools. Paved paths meandered through a variety of trees and shrubs, all clearly carefully chosen to create a stunning effect.

After a drive to the beach, where we found some unusual left-handed whelk and other shells, we came upon a Civil War lookout tower that was in surprisingly good condition. And at the end of the day we enjoyed a captivating conversation with the watchman, B. J. Rouse, who had fascinating stories to tell of the days when he had been the skipper of the Reynolds' ocean racing yachts, *Blitzen* and *Elizabeth McColl.* This wonderful stopover was one of the highlights of our east coast adventure, and to think we would have missed it if *Ern* had been a faster boat! Many years later the movie "*Cocoon*" was filmed in this spectacular location, and seeing it brought back many special memories.

A snowy egret enjoying Florida's sun

We were welcomed to Florida's balmy climate by a lovely variety of birds including snowy egrets and pelicans. The warm temperature was a welcome change from the chilly weather that had chased us down the coast, but pesky midges and noisy drum fish were the price paid for the luxury of being able to put away heavy sweaters and longjohns. One night we anchored in a niche just off the waterway and were wakened from a sound sleep by the pounding of powerful engines that seemed so close that we wondered if the anchor had dragged us into the channel. Peering out to check our position, we were met by the blinding beams of a searchlight as a huge tug gave two raucous blasts on the horn. We were relieved to realize he was requesting the attendant to open the next bridge, but our hearts continued to pound until we saw the dark form of the vessel pass on by and proceed down the channel.

A few days later we were treated to a complimentary night in a hotel owned by friends who thought we might appreciate a night ashore with a shower, flush toilets and other amenities not enjoyed on the boat. It was a generous gesture, but they failed to tell us that the hotel backed onto a railway line. At two o'clock in the morning a freight train came thundering down the tracks and woke us in terror and confusion. Charles practically threw me out of bed shouting,

"Get out of the way of the tug, it's getting closer!"

"Where is it? Where do I go?" I cried.

I thrashed about in terror trying to get out of the way of whatever was coming at us. Then we remembered that we were on land, and realized a train had passed by, and that we were perfectly safe. We tried to settle down, but sleep was no longer possible. We came to the conclusion that so-called restful nights ashore weren't always the best idea after all.

Charles and I had several discussions as to how the trip would proceed during the remainder of his leave of absence. I wanted to sail back to Vancouver via the Bahamas, across the Caribbean, through the Panama Canal, over to Hawaii and back to Vancouver. Charles preferred a leisurely cruise of the Bahamas followed by shipping *Ern* to the West Coast. Since shipping costs were excessive, we eventually decided we would try to sell her in Fort Lauderdale, where a typically persuasive yacht broker assured us he could sell her in a month. We left Miami for the Bahamas, with the intention of returning with a month to spare for *Ern* to be sold.

7   Turquoise Waters and White Beaches

The prospect of departing from Miami to start the crossing of the strong currents of the Gulf Stream rekindled the old excitement of leaving protected waters and embarking on new adventures, this time a cruise of the Bahamas.

Ern's crew

Fuel and provisions were topped up and we set off at midnight, after an unsuccessful attempt to catch a few hours of sleep. Crossing the Gulf Steam in order to make a landfall in Cat Cay in daylight was a test of *Ern*'s sea-kindly design, and she came up with flying colors. The required course kept the lights of Miami visible for much of the night, until the strong northerly current swept us to within the welcome sight of palm trees on the low-lying islands. Our arrival in shallower seas was announced by the color of the water as it changed from the deep blue of the Gulf Stream to a rich greenish-blue and finally a lovely apple green, with sea grass on the bottom swaying in the currents. Entry to the Bahamas was simple and trouble-free, and the setting of our courtesy flag of the Bahamas became a token of our "going foreign." Once again we enjoyed the instantaneous camaraderie with other sailors that is so much a part of the pleasure of cruising.

A load of grouper goes to market

It was here that we met two couples who stood out from all the rest. One couple, Alan and Sonja, were the best pair of sailors we'd met in our travels thus far. They had purchased a classic gaff-rigged ketch,

87

Autant, just for the trip. However, the engine was a disaster, difficult to start, then after a few minutes of operation, sputtering to a stop again. Their solution: they decided not to trifle with its cantankerous character, pulled it out, rearranged the ballast and sailed down the coast from New York without an engine. If they wanted to go ashore for provisions they would simply hail a tug and request a tow in and out of inlets as needed. When, early in the trip, the head became plugged, they simply decided to dispense with it as well and use a bucket! Though their choices were not what we would have made, we couldn't help but admire their pluck and determination.

The other couple, in their seventies, were sailing *Kon-Tiki,* a 30-foot trimaran, that they had built in the back yard of their estate in Connecticut. Frank was a retired vice-president of one of the largest corporations in the United States. Helen, his wife, who had been born with the proverbial "silver spoon in her mouth," recalled that even during the depression she had had a private nurse and all that money could buy. Yet in spite of their wealth they were a most down-to-earth couple, and though they found the trip tiring, they were thoroughly enjoying themselves. Helen, a beautiful lady with dancing brown eyes, was most sincere when she confided in a surprisingly deep voice, "What I like most about cruising is that all you need to concern yourself about are the basics—enough to eat, adequate clothing and knowing how to get where you're going safely. We're so glad to be rid of the trappings of so-called high society and jumping through the artificial hoops of propriety." How refreshing to hear this from people whose daily budget was enough to fund us for a week!

Before us lay the Grand Bahama Bank, with an average depth of about 30 feet and a distance of over 80 miles separating us from the next reference point at Northwest Passage. The irregular currents, combined with unmarked reefs, necessitated anchoring on the Bank at nightfall after a day's sail. However, being accustomed to cruising indented coastlines and waterways and enjoying the protection of countless coves and safe havens, my concept of an anchorage meant a protected cove or bay with little or no exposure to wind and wave.

It seemed preposterous that we were to anchor 40 miles from land, with nothing but undulating seas and a starry sky in sight. Yet here we were, setting the anchor in a vast area where depths average about 3 fathoms of bright, light green water so transparent that darting fish, clumps of coral, starfish and rocks were clearly visible. After setting the anchor we anxiously looked in all directions, as if land might miraculously appear in this immense region of shallow sea and sky. It was difficult to accept the reality of it all, and we sat in the cockpit a long time watching the stars appear, shining with that brightness that is only possible far away from lights and pollution. The cool evening blended into night and we reluctantly went below, for our next day promised to be a full one.

Sleep did not come easily, for the night still held some anxieties for us. *Ern* bobbed and jerked on the anchor rode as the wind ruffled the low swell then increased, causing the anchor rode to jerk and rattle in the fairlead. We frequently looked for a sign of dragging by checking our position relative to our companions anchored nearby. Why did that lazy half-moon seem to creep so slowly across the sky as it marked the reluctant passage of time of that endless night? At one point the anchor light on one of the other vessels went out, and as we peered into the semi-darkness an errant cloud blotted out the meager moon. Had their anchor dragged? Was the elderly couple in *Kon-Tiki* aware of the situation? Were they all right? Suddenly the moon burst forth from behind the cloud and the dark outline of their little trimaran was visible once more. God bless the moonlight, be it ever so hesitant. Slowly, ever so slowly the moon crept across the starry sky, giving way to a longed-for sunrise and a chance to resume our travels across the Grand Bahama Bank.

We arrived in Chub Cay the next day and, with northerly winds sweeping down from severe winter storms along the Atlantic seaboard, we were happy to stay for several days. This gave us time to walk the white coral and sand beaches, where we discovered the beauty of multi-colored and uniquely-shaped warm water seashells whose beauty contrasted so starkly with the dull grayish-white ones found in cold Pacific waters. Conchs were so plentiful on the beaches that they became a popular item on the menu and boaters created new recipes that were freely exchanged. We marveled at our ability to abandon our squeamishness as we detached the edible muscle from the slippery, slimy and unsightly remainder of the innards. Though this tough muscle had very little taste it was amazing how a variety of spices and thorough cooking could convert it into palatable, though still chewy, morsels.

Christmas street scene

The Christmas season in Nassau was the first any of our expanded group of cruising compatriots had spent away from the snow and cold of winters in the northern climes. As we sauntered down the streets in summer garb it seemed incongruous to see store displays of Santa and his reindeer flying over banks of cotton batting, and tiny Christmas trees sprayed with white frosting. Despite its strangeness for us, it was a Christmas long remembered as one of our happiest. Of the four cruising boats assembled in the anchorage, our table was the largest, so everyone joined us with a contribution to the meal. One boat had an oven so they roasted a small turkey complete with all the fixings; others brought veggies, dessert and the rest of the meal. Since we were all on a limited budget we exchanged gifts from spares we had on the boat, composed appropriate poems or created original art.

The following day was Junkanoo, a celebration featuring an exotic, spectacular parade of young and old, many in various stages of intoxication, but all ages enjoying themselves in their colorful and elaborate costumes, as they danced to the reverberating rhythms of the musicians, the drums usually overpowering the rest of the instruments. This exotic parade was a fitting ending to our most memorable merry Christmas.

We spent two glorious months cruising the Exumas and other islands of the Bahamas, a collage of great sailing and of anchorages where we marveled at the unbelievable beauty of the multi-hued colors of the water, especially at Warderick Wells and the safe coves where we could tuck ourselves in when northerly winds were predicted. We walked many miles on white and often deserted beaches, looking for shells, returning to *Ern* laden with our treasures. Going aground was a regular occurrence in the shoal, sandy waters, but we always managed to kedge ourselves off with no damage done, except perhaps to our pride. Charles reveled in fantastic snorkeling, but since I was a non-swimmer, I rowed the dinghy in the vicinity as an "escape boat" in case sharks were seen in the area.

One day Charles persuaded me to join him to see the wonderful variety of colors in a nearby coral formation. Wanting so much to share his pleasure, I tried, but I was so stressed by my fear of the water that instead of admiring the coral, I was mesmerized by the sight of the deep water beyond; to my regret I took only one or two very quick glances at the beautiful sight so close at hand, before scrambling back into the dinghy.

Warderick Wells panorama

On one occasion while visiting another boat in the anchorage where we had feasted on freshly caught fish, we decided to check on whether or not there were sharks in the area. We dropped the fish heads and guts overboard, and were astounded to see a 12-foot hammerhead shark appear from upstream in less than a minute. The speed with which the shark appeared was a shock, and we suddenly felt very vulnerable as we clambered into our little 8-foot dinghy for the row back to *Ern*. It was with genuine relief that we climbed on board and savored the welcoming safety of our boat. From then on, I was even happier to row around while Charles snorkeled with other boaters.

Local sloop approaching Nassau

As a cruising couple our relationship wasn't all peaches and cream, for although I was becoming more experienced as crew, my tendency to make suggestions was usually greeted with derision. When conning from the bow I could see the color of the bottom indicating shallower water before Charles could appreciate the difference in depth from the cockpit. Instead of accepting my advice as having some credence he would proceed on his set course until we ran aground. It was tempting to say, "I told you so," but by that time his mood was predictably angry, and besides, the bottom was soft sand and no harm was done. Generally, I kept my counsel and resorted to writing rebuttals in my diary.

Charles was a very bright person, but one of his permanent blind spots was not learning the terms "port" and "starboard." When anchoring, we often had sharp words when he would face forward and give verbal instructions that couldn't be heard from the cockpit, without using hand signals. He would angrily turn around and say, "Go to the right," or "Go to the left," leaving me in a quandary (and I usually did the wrong thing) for I didn't know if he meant the 'right' as he was facing the stern or if he meant the 'right' as he turned to face forward. Though we quietly chuckled when watching other boaters yelling at each other, usually as they tried to set the anchor, we also provided fellow sailors quite a few snickers as well.

Our funds were running low and the time for return was fast approaching, so we returned to the office of the boat broker in Fort Lauderdale, the one who had been so optimistic about selling *Ern* in "just a couple of weeks." But the reality was that fiberglass boats were taking over the market, and wooden vessels were passé. No one gave *Ern* a second look, let alone an offer. Consequently, we were forced to make arrangements to ship her to Vancouver by rail, the cheapest method available. Her mast was hauled and she was loaded onto a sturdy custom-built cradle and placed on a flatbed for the long trip to her new home.

Once more we were forced to return to reality. Our funds were running low and it was time to get back to work. Perhaps now was the time to "become normal" again, settle down, live in a house and start a family.

Nassau waterfront market

8   Return to the West Coast

For our return to the west coast, we bought an old Chevrolet station wagon for $125 and loaded as much of our belongings as possible onto double roof racks. There was just enough space left for Beau to curl up in the back seat amidst the tightly packed sails, boxes of seashells and personal items. Our vehicle, a faded blue remnant of an earlier period of the automobile industry, had dents and rust spots and peeled paint, but as long as it could be coaxed into running it was fine by us. With a month left before Charles was scheduled to return to work, we set off in our tired and overloaded relic.

The change from traveling for five months at an average speed of five knots to driving along busy highways at 60 to 70 miles per hour took some adjustment. We realized we had felt much safer on the boat, where approaching vessels generally moved at a leisurely pace and we had plenty of time to react to their movements. But in highway traffic we felt exposed and vulnerable to the variations of skill, attention and sobriety of other drivers on the road. However, within a few days of driving in traffic we adjusted and began to relax.

With skillful persuasion we managed to nurse the old vehicle across the southern United States and head north, with no major expenses other than a couple of tune-ups and four new tires. The speedometer didn't work, but we succeeded in making the trip without receiving any speeding tickets—probably because the car was so overloaded and the engine so old that there was little likelihood that we would reach the speed limit, let alone exceed it!

In Oregon however, our luck ran out when we stopped at a roadside park to give Beau a needed walk. The road in the park wound among lovely big cedars and had several sharp speed bumps. Though we were moving at a snail's pace one brutal speed bump jolted the car so sharply that the weight on the heavily loaded roof rack partially collapsed the roof, and we were startled by the threatening sound of bending metal. We both looked up to see if the roof was about to collapse on our heads, and in that split-second interval the forward movement of the car brought us into collision with a huge cedar. The motor stopped, steam spewing from the collapsed radiator.

"Damn, double damn," was all we could say, for so close to home it seemed a dreadful waste to take the time and money to repair our ailing, worthless vehicle. Fortunately, a sympathetic old man towed us to an auto wrecker in the vicinity, who was able to make the necessary repairs to get the engine running. We looked a fine sight, for now the hood was so dented that it wouldn't close properly, but slanted upward at a rakish angle. Undeterred, our scruffy, good natured repairman looped a tattered rope around the errant hood and tied it to the front bumper declaring, "There you are, good as new!"

As our funds were severely depleted, we were very keen to get back to Canada, so we drove on until we reached the border some time after midnight. It's a wonder we were let in, for not only did we have a wreck of a car that was loaded with gear, but we were exhausted, our eyes were bloodshot from a prolonged day's drive and even Beau was looking scruffy and tired. But luck was with us for the Canada Custom's officer was in a good mood and met us with a cheery,

"How are you tonight?"

"We're just returning from a long trip and we had some car problems but...."

"Welcome back to Canada," he interrupted, "Have a good night!"

What a relief not to have to unpack and go through our bulging boxes and bags in our exhausted condition! Home, sweet home at last.

Meanwhile, *Ern* had arrived at the rail yards in New Westminster just two days before we crossed the border into Canada. When we went to see her we were shocked to see the condition of the sturdy cradle— the 4" x 4" timber that had been across her bow was broken, metal rods along her sides were bent, and her supports were cobbled up with some shabby looking repairs that somehow held up. Clearly, since leaving Florida, her rail car had been shunted violently down a siding and had come to such an abrupt halt as to do untold damage to the cradle supporting her.

Prior to leaving Fort Lauderdale we had been warned that hobos would likely break into *Ern* while she waited on railway sidings for the next train going along the desired route. As predicted, the lock had indeed been sawn through and she had been broken into, but since we had removed everything before shipping her there was nothing to steal. Strangely, the vibration of travel by rail had shaken the stove to bits, and pieces were found scattered throughout the boat, in the forward cabin, in the bilges and even behind the engine.

Charles returned to work and we made arrangements for a fisherman to tow *Ern* from New Westminster for the short trip back to the same docks in Annacis Slough we had left several years previously on our ill-fated trip with *Kakoodlak*. A crane lowered her to the muddy Fraser River and I went aboard. Knowing that her wooden hull would weep some moisture after being dried out for a month, I was prepared to do some pumping until the planks swelled up and the seams became tight again. But to my surprise, the water was streaming in at such a rate that I had to pump continuously to keep water from covering the floorboards. I ran up to the yard office before the crane had departed and looked for the foreman.

"She's taking on water at a terrible rate. Can you get the crane to raise her again until we see what's wrong?" I pleaded.

"Don't worry, lady, she's been out of the water for a month. You can expect that to happen for a while."

His condescending tone made me angry but I didn't have time to argue.

"No, it's coming in too fast for just dried out planks! I've got to go back and pump before the floorboards are awash."

I ran down to the boat, pumped hard for a few minutes and was just able to contain the flow before returning to the office once more.

"You've got to lift her, she's still taking on too much water," I snapped.

"Relax lady, you've got to accept the fact that she's a dry boat."

"I know she's dry, but we've had wooden boats out of the water for a month before and they haven't leaked like this. I've got to go!"

A third time I asked for help but this time the foreman just interrupted,

"For gawd's sake, just pump a little longer and she'll be OK. Don't get so worried, dearie." That condescending "dearie" piqued my ire but I didn't have time for a satisfying reply, and once more ran back to *Ern*.

Back at the boat I saw Scottie, our fisherman friend, pulling up to the dock. I ran to him and told him my dilemma with the excessive water pouring into *Ern*. Predictably, he replied,

"Ah, don't worry, Margo, she's been out of the water for a month. She'll need some time for the planks to swell up and close the seams."

I resigned myself to having no one listen to me, and tied *Ern* up alongside for the tow to the fisherman's marina. The main bilge pump, mounted on deck, was a type that required vertical pumping. By now my muscles were protesting furiously, for I had been pumping steadily for almost an hour. I had no choice but to keep pumping, all the time complaining and muttering about the amount of water coming in, when finally Scottie said,

"Gawd, she's takin' in a helluva lot of water—you've got a problem!"

"That" I shouted, "is what I've been trying to tell someone for the last hour, but no one would listen to me!"

As soon as *Ern* was tied to the dock I ran to the office and borrowed an electric pump and was finally able to take a rest. I phoned Charles at work and he asked the inevitable question,

"Is *Ern* in the water? Is she weeping much?"

"Yes, she's in the water, and she's not just weeping, she's sobbing uncontrollably."

"Remember, Margo she's dry and will be taking...." Before he could finish the sentence I interrupted, "Don't tell me about taking on water. It's pouring in so fast I've had to borrow an electric pump. We've got to haul her for there is a steady stream coming in from the bow."

That afternoon I had her hauled and the problem immediately became evident. When she had been flung down the siding with enough force to break the 4" x 4" stud the caulking had jarred loose, creating open gaps that allowed water to enter freely. When repairs were completed we finally moored her in a marina, while we moved back into our house.

Returning to life ashore and the routine of the workaday world was a necessity at this point, for we were broke. The sorting and identification of the hundreds of colorful shells we had collected brought back fond memories as we tried to settle down once more, and our thoughts now turned to having a family.

At that time, Thursday editions of the *Vancouver Sun* newspaper featured a full page of photographs of some of the many infants then available for adoption. In 1967 birth control was hush-hush and abortions were a crime, so there were many unwanted infants brought into the world. I was saddened to think of children being placed in foster and group homes where their environment and individual care would likely be much less than we could provide. Eventually we made a decision, and adopted a six-week old boy, Devereau.

However, the adoption of a little girl had to be postponed as a result of shocking health news. Only those who have heard the dreaded diagnosis of cancer can relate to the terror and agonizing worry that is suffered with this terrible disease. Many sleepless nights found me tossing and turning, worrying and wondering if this was Fate's way of punishing me for causing my parents so much pain. Grey hair became noticeable though I was only in my mid-thirties.

The day before my operation I deliberately checked in late to reduce the time spent in the hospital's cold, intimidating walls. After a bland dinner, I went to a patio and gazed at the view across Vancouver's inner harbor. Leaning over to look at the flower garden below I braced myself on the railing.

"Don't jump! it's a long way down!"

"I'm not going to jump, besides I wouldn't want to mess up the blossoms."

Two nurses escorted me back to the ward with my arms securely held.

"The patio is out of bounds after 7 p.m. We looked all over for you. You shouldn't have been out there!"

The next morning as I was wheeled to the operating room a nurse asked if I was Margo Wood. "No." I lied. Soon my doctor appeared and asked why I was denying my name.

"I wanted to speak to you and settle something before the operation. When you open me up I want you to give me your word that if I'm full of cancer you'll find a way to end it all then and there. I don't want to be told that I have two or three years to live in agony before I die. Give me your word."

"I can't do that."

"Give me your word," I shouted.

"All right Margo, all right, it will be all right."

Following the operation, I drove home in a joyful yet pensive mood. *I've come fact-to-face with my mortality. Until now I've ignored such considerations but from now on I've got to make each and every day count 110%. I don't want the "what ifs" to accumulate so that when I'm an old lady I'll feel that I've just been a spectator.*

Surgery and a period of recuperation did the trick, and six months later we adopted Charmian, a tiny five-and-a-half pound girl, just 11 days old. But it was five long years involving regular check-ups before I was given the "all-clear" report by the doctor.

Charmian and Devereau

Naturally our lives changed dramatically with the addition of children, and for a few years our two-week vacations were limited to revisiting favorite cruising areas on the British Columbia coast. Another major change was my realization that I had new responsibilities on board. As one friend pointedly asked,

"What are you going to do if one of your children falls overboard when you're sailing, stand and yell for Charles?"

Prairie style swimming lessons

I realized I had to deal with my fear of water, and signed up for a class with the title, "Beginners' Swimming for the Last Time." The ungainly instructor had a Yasser Arrafat beard and was dressed in baggy pants and a faded T-shirt with a tear at the shoulder. When he shuffled along the side of the pool to meet our little class I thought maybe he was the janitor, until he started to talk in voice so quiet that we had to strain our ears to hear him yet with the authority of one who knows his job. A discerning psychologist, he searched out our personalities and dealt with each of us individually as he put us through the painful process of overcoming our fear of water. He joked with one, hypnotized another, teased two of the women, and he challenged me. He discovered what made each of us tick and worked us with a prod of the pole or a timely comment until we all succeeded in learning to swim. Later, I continued with lessons, and eventually was able to join Charles in obtaining SCUBA diving certification.

The division of labor that Charles and I had followed had altered only slightly during our years of cruising. As had been our habit, Charles looked after navigation, the engine, sails and electrical gear, and I was responsible for provisioning, cooking, cleaning and storekeeping, and we now shared taking care of the children. I was the monkey that jumped ashore when docking and the one in the cockpit taking orders from the Captain on the foredeck. I didn't plan, I reacted.

But then a major and very fortunate change in my knowledge and confidence occurred as a result of our joining a yacht club to take advantage of convenient moorage. I became a member of the ladies' sailing group. Starting with Flying Juniors and progressing to Cal 20s, Cal 28s and Thunderbirds, we eventually had the fun of competing in Adam's Cup eliminations in the Pacific Northwest.

The racing team in Portland, Oregon

For the first time in my sailing life I was no longer limited to the cockpit following the captain's instructions. Here I was working on the foredeck while crewing with women who discussed strategy, wind, currents and every aspect of making the boat travel faster. This was hands-on, in-the-water education in boat handling, and it taught me a great deal. I had spent more time cruising than any of the rest of the gang, but from racing experience they knew a lot more than I about trimming sails and working the boat efficiently. It was a first-class learning experience that gave me increased confidence in boats and in myself, one I would recommend to any woman who plans to spend time on the water.

Meanwhile during the nine years since our marriage, news of my parents had come to me from one of our neighbors, though I always sent a card and letter sharing our activities every Christmas. Upon learning that we had adopted our children the barriers to communication were eliminated. My parents no longer feared that any children of our union would be "social misfits." There was a reconciliation of sorts, and we visited back and forth until my parents passed away.

What pain discrimination can cause, whether racial, religious, or some other irrational basis. For nine long years my parents' intransigence had caused them the loss of a daughter, a loss I felt just as keenly. I had longed to share tales of my travels with my parents who had been literally chained to a life of endless hard work on the farm. It could have been so exciting for them to have followed the adoption process and been present when we first brought Devereau home. But these wonderful moments with my family could never be resurrected. My mother only lived to see Charmian's third birthday, and although my father lived much longer, a truly positive relationship between Charles and him never became a reality. Life is too short to destroy precious years because of such intolerance and fearfulness.

An outcome of our struggle with my cancer, together with the sadness we felt over relations with my parents, was that we were faced inexorably with the fact of our mortality. Was living a "normal existence," jumping through the hoops of going to work for a paycheck and marching in step to social protocol all there was to life? Wasn't there was more to it than that? Still in search of adventure in our lives, we realized we wanted to continue cruising. We would live our lives to the full and share this joy with our children, but to do so we would need a larger boat.

With regret, we put *Ern* on the market, and within a short time she was sold to a young sailor who admired her lines and well-maintained appearance. I cried bitter tears as *Ern* left the dock and sailed away with her new owner, for she represented so many happy times and rich experiences. Saying good-by seemed like closing the door on an old friend; she wasn't just the proverbial "hole in the water where you pour money." She was a reliable partner who shared exciting adventures as she took us in good weather and bad to safe anchorages and forgave us for the buckets of foul-smelling water spilled on her decks when cleaning the rotted innards of beautiful shells. Her mahogany always glowed with the richness and warmth only to be seen on freshly varnished wood. She was the best.

Shore leave

9   *Frodo*

After studying various designs and visiting several boatyards, we decided to invest in a Spencer 51 hull, with the intention of designing and constructing an interior that would make her a livable family cruising boat. It was fun to plan with so much more interior space available than we had experienced in previous boats. We took delivery of the hull complete with major bulkheads, floorboards and an Izuzu diesel engine installed. Having worked in Alexander Stephens' Shipyard in Glasgow from the ground up, Charles was competent to deal with all aspects of wiring and plumbing, in addition to the woodworking experience he had gained on our previous vessels.

If all went as planned, we would at last achieve our long-cherished dream of sailing around the world, this time with our young family. We hoped to have the boat ready for sea in three or four years, as Charles was continuing employment as a mechanical engineer and could work on the boat only in his spare time. While the children were attending school I was able to do odd jobs on the boat such as installing the ceiling liner and trim, sanding and oiling teak fittings, and being a general helper. Our life was back on track again, and we eagerly looked forward to the time when our boat would be ready to go to sea and our next venture would begin.

But once again, Fate stepped in with a vengeance, and suddenly our world was turned upside-down. At 49 years of age, Charles was stricken with a major heart attack following what had appeared to be a one-week case of heartburn. I had convinced Charles that it seemed serious and could indicate a heart problem, so the doctor checked him over. Unfortunately the doctor agreed with Charles' self-diagnosis and sent him home with the advice to eat only bland foods and "take it easy." Two days later Charles was rushed to the hospital in extreme pain, suffering from a major heart attack. He remained in intensive care for 10 days, followed by 6 weeks in the regular ward. At one point I had asked the doctor what his chances were, for he was dreadfully weak and barely able to whisper. The doctor's reply was, "Toss a coin; he isn't a smoker, he doesn't drink, he isn't overweight and he has age on his side. That's all I can say."

How devastating to be faced with the possibility of his passing at such a stage in our lives. At that time the song "Delta Dawn" was played regularly on local radio stations and as I drove home from the hospital the lyrics, "And did I hear you say he was meeting you here today to take you to his mansion in the sky," became a litany which to this day is still a reminder of the terrible time we spent, uncertain of his recovery. Charles did not make a full recovery, for his stamina and endurance never returned to the level of well-being he had enjoyed prior to this set-back.

Why don't doctors warn family members about the psychological side effects that a heart attack or an accident can have on the victim and on the family? I was prepared for Charles to come home from the hospital in a weakened condition, and that a return even to a diminished level of his former strength and health would be a lengthy process. But I wasn't ready for the change in personality that occurred. Instead of being fairly easy to live with, he became an irritable and impatient stranger, who lost much of his interest in being a father and became self-centered and detached. I couldn't do anything to please him. If he wanted toast at breakfast it was either too well done or not done enough, had too much butter or too little. Life with him became almost unbearable and I felt sorry for the children, who didn't under-

107

stand his irritability. I rationalized that he was probably feeling angry that such a cruel blow had been dealt to his health, and since there was no one else he could verbally strike out at, I, being closest, received the brunt of his frustration.

At times I felt trapped, partly because of the demands of our young children and partly because the boat was becoming a financial burden and we had only begun to purchase material and equipment needed to finish the project. I wanted to run away, but I couldn't face the prospect of "kicking a man when he's down," nor could I imagine walking out and leaving the children with him or running away with them. I didn't want to make a move that would give my parents the opportunity to smugly say, "We told you so." It was a very difficult time, and my hair became grayer with each passing month. Then slowly, ever so slowly, Charles regained a modicum of health, though he was advised not to return to the stresses of his occupation as an engineer. There was nothing else for it but for me to return to teaching in order to maintain a positive cash flow and to complete the purchase of equipment for the boat, for our dream was still alive.

Crash! - The day of the launch

And then, after three years of work, came the exciting culmination: the day of the launch. It was June 1975 when I christened our boat *Frodo*. We were relieved that we had been able to finish her to our satisfaction in spite of the health problems that had extended the planned date of launching by a year. *Frodo* was a striking, skipper-blue center-cockpit sloop, that turned out to be easily handled and a great performer.

Of course as a result of Charles' heart attack we had adjusted our plans somewhat. It was uncertain how his body would stand up to the rigors of overnight sailing, along with the added responsibility of taking a young family to sea. However, because we had finished construction of *Frodo* under a manufacturer's license, it was necessary to export her within 6 months of launching to avoid being liable for the taxes on her equipment and on the labor we had expended. We couldn't afford to keep her and sail her in Canada, yet the dream of sailing around the world was now beyond our physical capabilities.

We knew compromises may have to be made in our cherished travel plans, but were not sure just what would be possible. Our first choice would be a cruise to Mexico and Polynesia, but if need be we could limit our trip to coastal travel in Mexico and then sell the boat in San Diego. However, if the trip to San Francisco proved to be too exhausting for Charles we would simply sell *Frodo* there and once more, abandon our dream.

With these realities clearly in mind but always hoping for the best, we gathered a crew of five friends and departed from Vancouver on a sunny, windy afternoon. We had barely cleared the bell buoy when Charles became seasick. Here we go again, for in the excitement of departure he had forgotten to put on his Scopolamine ear patches. Armed with the patches, we were ready to set off again the next morning, and the trip proceeded without problems to Victoria and Neah Bay before heading southward to San Francisco.

After our previous experience off Cape Mendocino we warned the crew to be prepared for possible rough weather in its vicinity. Sure enough, traveling about 30 miles offshore we were overtaken by sudden, very strong winds that brought our speed above the 17-knot maximum of our speedometer. After double-reefing the main I went forward to help the two strongest members of the crew to drop the foresail and rig the storm jib while Charles remained at the wheel. (Self-furling headsails were not developed until several years later.) Several large breaking seas came aboard as we worked the foredeck but we were secured with safety harness and the job was done without difficulty.

Upon returning to the cockpit my hand seemed to be catching on my cuff, nicking my finger. Glancing down, I was surprised to see that the diamond in my engagement ring had been torn from the setting while I helped to control the thrashing headsail. Clearly it had been washed overboard in the melee. I was reminded of Guy de Maupassant's short story and wondered if by chance a fish might swallow my diamond, be caught by a poor fisherman and give him a story to tell for years to come.

Happiness is . . .

My next watch proved to be interesting. After several hours of heavy seas and gusty blasts the wind dropped and we motored through disturbed waters with a steadying sail to ease the motion. I was on the wheel with a young member of the crew when suddenly a ball of light as intense as the spotlight of a ship approached from dead ahead. It briefly disappeared from sight as a high swell hid it from view only to reappear larger and closer, dead ahead, bearing down on us with dreadful accuracy.

Collisions at sea are usually deadly, especially for the smaller vessel, and since we had seen several huge, rusty Russian factory boats in the previous 48 hours my first thought was of one of them running down on us. I flung open the hatch and flew below to the control panel to switch on the strobe light, hoping to warn the approaching vessel of our presence. Obviously, it had not noticed our running lights and was continuing on a collision course. I was overcome with horror until suddenly I realized that this blazing ball of light was in fact a lustrous, full moon rising on our disheveled horizon. What a wonderful moment of recognition—there was my old friend from years gone by! What a resounding relief! The moon was a beautiful sight for the rest of the night, and when the watch changed I was able to laugh as I told the crew of our close encounter with a celestial object!

Approaching Golden Gate Bridge

Upon arrival in San Francisco we moored in Sausalito in order to have a quiet locale for our headquarters rather than tying up in busy, noisy downtown San Francisco. The wife of one of the crew flew from Vancouver with Devereau and Charmian, making it a great reunion for all, and we decided to celebrate and give the children a treat by visiting the park on Angel Island, the former Immigration and Quarantine Station in the middle of San Francisco Bay. We tied to the last remaining mooring in the bay, and went off for a picnic in the park. By the time we returned to the boat the afternoon breeze had picked up and became quite gusty.

Several sailors were showing off their machismo attitude by sailing through the moored fleet, stalling their vessels into the wind then spinning around and dashing off at random. Suddenly a gust caught one show-off by surprise, and before he could react, his 26-foot Excalibur sloop hit us bow-on our midship section, puncturing a 3-inch hole in our shiny blue hull and snapping off his own bow fitting. The shocking thud brought us forth ready for action, only to see him sailing away. I yelled at him and obtained his name and telephone number as he proceeded on his way. We were incredulous that a fellow boater could arrogantly sail off after causing a collision without returning to apologize and provide insurance information. After collecting the names and addresses of some willing witnesses we ate dinner and settled down for the night, with plans to return to Sausalito the next day. But Fate was ready to play more tricks on us.

At midnight Charles was awakened by a change in the motion of the boat. He looked out and saw to his astonishment that *Frodo* was hauled off at an angle to the moorings by a tremendous current flowing through the bay. He dashed below, quickly putting on his gear. "Get up, Margo, we're going to drag at any moment!"

Just then the boat lurched as we began to drag the mooring towards the shore. Charles turned on the engine and I immediately let go the lines tied to the mooring buoy and we headed back to Sausalito. After entering Richardson Bay Charles put the engine out of gear and we drifted as he got his bearings, sorting out the maze of onshore lights, buoys and illuminated navigational aids. Then, as he put the engine into gear it promptly died. This wasn't supposed to happen, what else could go wrong? Thinking that the idling speed was too slow (although there had been no indication of this previously) Charles went below and set the idling speed higher. The engine roared at idling speed but when put into gear it died again. He re-started the engine several times and each time it ran smoothly in neutral only to stop when put into gear. We were perplexed, for the engine had functioned perfectly up to this time. Fortunately, the children slept through our dilemma, but our bleary-eyed crew wandered on deck and asked what was wrong. We couldn't tell them, for we didn't know, but we began to suspect that the propeller had somehow become fouled.

By now we had gone aground on the same hump in the middle of the channel that we had encountered on our approach a few days earlier. This time it was in the dead of night with no one about, so we decided that the only thing to do was to kedge out an anchor, set up an anchor watch and sort things out in the morning. Eventually the tide floated us off and we pulled up to our anchor. But our private gremlin had not left us, for the engine still refused to turn the propeller when put into gear. By now we were certain that something had fouled the propeller. Charles went to the engine room to adjust the idling screw, but the wrench slipped out of his hand. It slid towards the bilge and then, as luck would have it, it hung up across the only two uninsulated wiring points in the whole engine room, those of the oil pressure switch, which had been spared his fussy attention because of its awkward position.

Sparks flew, the wires rapidly grew white hot and the insulation melted and burned. The acrid smell of an electrical short filled the engine room and spread throughout the boat while I ran for the fire extinguisher. Charles tore the wires loose, killing the fire and stopping the short. One of the crew rushed to the engine room, looking pale and distraught, eyes bulging out and with a quivering voice queried,

"Does this happen very often when cruising?"

Trying to be nonchalant I replied, "Oh, there's the odd day that things go wrong, but Charles has it under control. While he cleans up and rewires the engine let's have a cup of coffee."

By this time the children were up.

"Where's the fire?"

"What's that awful smell?"

"What's happening?"

Herding everyone to the galley I made breakfast and attempted to calm them all down. When the re-wiring job was complete and we were anchored well off the channel Charles and I donned our wet suits. Charles dove first but in his haste he hadn't tightened up his weight belt sufficiently and it slipped off into the water. As he suddenly surfaced, cursing and spluttering, he tore off his facemask with its expensive prescription lens and it, too, flipped off and sank in the murky water. Could anything else go wrong?

Now it was my turn to check the propeller. What I saw was a white, cocoon-like sheet wrapped around the propeller and floating like a wraith in the water. This was the first time I had dived alone and I was tense as I hacked away with my diving knife at the tough wrapping on the propeller. I was almost finished when urgent tugs on the signal rope interrupted the job. I surfaced and took a rest while a member of the crew dove in to finish the job. The offending gremlin turned out to be a jib from a small boat. Someone had laid it out to dry on the dock only to have it blown into the water, where it sank. Once we were mobile again, we went to a yard to have our puncture repaired. Unfortunately, we were constantly reminded of our bewitched trip to Angel

Island, for the yard was unable to match the exact shade of blue of the gelcoat and as it weathered, the ugly patch became clearly evident. Although Charles didn't say anything positive to me at the time, he later wrote in the log,

"I'm lucky that Margo handles these occasional hectic moments with phlegmatic calm." It would have been nice if he had given me a pat on the back at the time but that wasn't his style. It was many years later that I read the log and picked up the compliment.

It was a South Pole explorer who said that no one would be interested in any expedition where everything went without a hitch, and that it was the accidents and vicissitudes of a trip that were of interest to others. Forget interesting tales for others, we would have been perfectly happy to have foregone the eventful chain of events that bedeviled our Angel Island excursion.

We were delighted to leave San Francisco and proceed southward, making daily runs from place to place so we could visit as many ports as possible and give everyone interesting stop-overs along the way. Following a visit to Morro Bay we motored some 15 miles off the California coast between Morro Bay and Point Conception. Here we saw one of the most fascinating displays of nature we had ever experienced at sea. On this cool, extremely foggy and windless night a gentle swell caressed the ocean's surface. The heavy fog blotted out the night sky, while the running lights cast an eerie glow. The crew was anxious and on deck, partly out of concern for travel in such poor visibility and partly to help identify the direction of sound from any vessels in the vicinity.

Soon our spirits were lifted as some dolphins joined us. Regardless of the number of times one revels in the sight of dolphins merrily swimming and diving alongside a boat, they are always a joy to behold. We watched the phosphorescent tracks criss-crossing our path and leaving a trail of sparkling "fairy dust" in their wake. Then suddenly a line of bright water appeared, running perpendicular to our line of travel and extending off into the distance on either side of *Frodo*. At first we thought it was a whale or a submarine crossing our bows and we became quite concerned at the close proximity of such a large entity. Reducing our speed we listened intently for any unusual sounds while we searched the restricted circle of visibility for a glimpse of approaching danger. Yet there was no change in the state of the sea as we crossed the clear-cut line between the black sea and the band of light.

Soon more bands of underwater lights appeared, about 20 feet wide and separated from each other by dark seas every few hundred yards, and we crossed them in succession. The fog lifted slightly and we could see the light bands further ahead and for some distance on either side. They were not perfectly regular, sometimes curving and taking a jog, but always the transition of dark to light was clear.

Over the next three hours we passed over band after band. The dolphins continued to accompany us and their fiery trails traced a squiggle of light across the bands of light and dark with complete abandon. The bands of light* appeared to get brighter as the night advanced, as though they approached the surface and later receded, becoming less intense as dawn approached. Towards morning the gaps of darkness became larger and the lights gradually faded until they were no longer visible. Though at first we had been apprehensive, our feelings of confusion turned to awe at the unforgettable sight we had been privileged to witness.

As our trip along the coast progressed, it became apparent that overnight trips were simply too demanding for Charles to handle. Although he would not complain, there were times when he was clearly uncomfortable and he would unconsciously rub his chest in the

---

Upon researching the history of the phenomenon known as "sea lights" we found it to be a rare form of bioluminescence made by millions of dinoflagellates. At that time there were only a limited number of observations documented, occurring in widely separated locations. The lights have been variously described as "powerful beams of light directed upwards from under water," "bright shoal water," "luminous wheels of lights" and "rivers of fire."

vicinity of his heart. Some days there would be a gray pallor to his complexion, usually accompanied by a straightening of the soft, natural wave in his hair. He didn't argue when I suggested that perhaps we should limit our travel plans to a Mexican cruise and then sell *Frodo* in southern California.

San Diego marked the end of the second phase of our voyage and proved to be a friendly city with many interesting spots to visit. We enjoyed the warmth of the sun that was a pleasant change from the cool winds and fog we had experienced along much of the coast; it was an enjoyable stop-over for all of us.

San Simeon Bay welcoming party

10   Mexico Ole!

The first part of our Mexico trip brought us to San Diego, a pleasant cruise that brought several surprises. Here we stayed for six weeks to wait out the Mexican hurricane season and to get the children, now in Grades 2 and 3, started on their correspondence courses. Our young crew left for Polynesia and a friend joined us in December to continue the trip.

While in San Diego we had some interesting conversations with cruisers about the anchorages and ports along the Mexican mainland coast. A few had made sketches they shared with us and by the time we departed we had several different versions of attractive spots that gave some hints as to what lay before us.

When we set forth once again it was with the anticipation that comes with the prospect of exploring a country not previously visited. Our southbound trip along the Baja peninsula was punctuated by a series of interesting, rolly anchorages bordering the scenic coast, where cacti towered on the dry slopes and marine life provided constant fascination. *Frodo* performed well, and the prevailing northwesterly winds and southerly current moved us along comfortably. Each day the trip was enriched by the detailed information gleaned from the classic reference, *Baja Sea Guide, Volume II* by Leland R. Lewis, which we took turns reading aloud along the way.

Until this trip we had not had any experience going ashore in a dinghy through surf. Our first venture was in Bahia Thurloe, just south of Turtle Bay, a popular stop for coastal cruisers. A brisk southerly wind added to the slight swell that landed on the far shore, and as we viewed the wave action from windward it appeared to be a reasonably safe and trouble-free operation. Our approach was innocent enough, and seemed to be working fine when suddenly we were unceremoniously flipped over by a breaking wave. We struggled to our feet to find ourselves waist-high in the warm, ruffled water and the dinghy overturned. Suddenly we realized that our spindly 7-year-old daughter, Charmian, was nowhere to be seen—she had literally disappeared into thin air! There was only one place to look, so we quickly turned the dinghy over and there she was, calmly gazing up at us. What a brave little soul! Our only casualties were a pair of lost sunglasses and some very soggy sandwiches.

Charmian gaining experience at the helm

After that we paid much more attention to wave action, secured our lunches in waterproof containers and tied our sunglasses about our necks. Then we made a practice of watching the Mexican fishermen as they deftly brought their pangas through the surf, and tried to imitate their well-timed actions. It took some time and a few wet landings, but we gradually developed enough skill that shore trips became enjoyable challenges.

Our visit to Cabo San Lucas was a page from the past, for at that time it was little more than a sleepy fishing village, only just starting to become aware of tourism. Cabo then had a bakery, three hotels, a grocery store, Port Captain, Immigration and Customs Offices, and some small shops. The long beach fronting the bay was empty, apart from a few cantinas and the odd fisherman's shack. Everyone we met along the dusty streets made eye contact as we exchanged smiling greetings of "Buenos dias" and "Buenas tardes." When I entered the bakery a chicken walking along the counter was unceremoniously shooed off by the laughing Mexican lady, and just then a pig wandered in the back door! It was an unforgettable sight though at the time we hardly noticed it because of the wonderful smell of fresh-baked bolillos, (large, delicious Mexican buns) and sugared cookies that lined the shelves.

Following a quick trip to La Paz for Christmas and a change of crew, we planned to begin our visit of the mainland. In order to travel the shortest distance while crossing the Sea of Cortez we retraced our route to Los Frailes and anchored. There we enjoyed several trips ashore to hike and collect shells and some exhilarating swimming and body surfing. The next day we set our sails and headed for Isla Isabela roughly 100 miles distant across the Sea of Cortez. We looked forward to a rollicking sail to the island, but unfortunately after a short period the wind dropped, forcing us to motor for the best part of the over-night passage.

At sunrise we saw a clear profile of the island, yet we knew it was many miles distant. After the sun rose higher in the sky and the silhouette disappeared, we realized that the refraction of the early morning light had provided us with a tantalizing preview. We arrived at midday, anchored, took an easy row to shore and hiked up to the top of the ridge overlooking the anchorage. What an incredible variety of seabirds inhabited this wild and rugged island! Some time later Jacques Cousteau filmed a documentary in this special place and named it as one of his favorite spots in the world.

A wild and sleepless night followed. The surf broke and gurgled loudly on the port side reefs and ledges of the southern anchorage while on the starboard side the regular, vibrating crash of the southerly swell as it was hurled into huge weathered sea caves combined to make unbelievable sound effects. Added to this was the ga-dug, ga-dug, of the anchor chain as it bounced across the rock-strewn bottom.

How could anyone sleep? As the tide rose and fell and *Frodo* swung at her mooring, the sounds from the crashing swell became louder and closer one minute, then more distant as the breakers swished and muttered on the rocky ledges. While Charles slept, I was up and down like a groundhog, checking to see if the anchor had dragged each time the sound effects changed.

Frodo's crew on shore leave

Our cruise along the mainland was a leisurely trip punctuated by shore excursions so the family could explore the beach, swim, collect shells and visit small villages along the way. We thrilled to the sighting of marine life we had not seen before such as sunfish, turtles, sharks and whales. Everyone marveled at seeing beautiful royal terns with their elegant long tail feathers, thieving frigate birds, saucy yellow, orange and blue-footed boobies and rare fish-eating bats. Fishing was excellent, and trading for lobster and shrimp provided a pleasant change of menu from the regular fare.

Landing a yellowtail

Just for "something to do," as we cruised the coast Charles sketched land profiles and the shape and location of anchorages we visited. When we approached an anchorage I would take the helm and in just a few minutes he would create a rough drawing of the offshore view, any significant landmarks and the configuration of the bay. Having an artistic bent as well as an engineer's attention to detail, he was able to produce sketches that were noticeably more accurate than any we had been given in San Diego.

After a trip to the mainland and north into the Sea of Cortez we returned to La Paz, where a family of four joined us for the return trip to San Diego known as the "Baja Bash." It was established that the guests would share in keeping the boat tidy and washing and drying the dishes.

Since their two teen-aged children had had no experience aboard a boat they were cautioned about many things, including not using large amounts of toilet paper in the head. It was explained that there was a curve in the hose exiting the head and that one of our previous crew had put Kleenex in the head, plugging the hose. To remove the plugged material Charles disconnected the hose, attached a portable bilge pump and used backpressure to eliminate the plugged material. When the pressure blew out the offending Kleenex and other material it had resulted in the entire surfaces of the bathroom being splattered with brown, gooey gobs that I scraped off and scrubbed.

To avoid repeating such an unpleasant cleaning job in the future, Charles devised a plan whereby any material plugging the hose could be captured in a plastic bag. The person who had plugged the hose with overly generous supplies of toilet paper would hold the bag while Charles used a portable pump to apply backpressure to clear the system. Bobby, the 17-year old boy who had just won a scholarship to a prestigious American university, listened to the warning about the head with a sardonic expression; his younger sister quietly giggled.

As the arduous trip northward from Cabo San Lucas progressed, it became evident that Bobby was not doing his share to help with life aboard. He would leave his clothes scattered in the main cabin and regularly avoided drying dishes when it was his turn. I found his lack of cooperation quite annoying and made some subtle hints that he studiously ignored. Part way through the trip his mother and I were chatting in the main cabin as we tidied up after the evening meal when suddenly Bobby burst in from the forward cabin looking pale and horrified.

"What's the matter, Bobby dear?" his doting mother asked.

"Mom, I've plugged the head, I've plugged the head!"

I was delighted, for it couldn't happen to a more deserving person! Perhaps my voice had a slight tinge of victory in it as I called to Charles who was in the aft cabin,

"Guess what, honey, Bobby plugged the head."

"I'll get the pump in a minute. Margo, have we got a good plastic bag, preferably a strong one?" said Charles with a twinkle in his eye as he entered the salon.

Soon the three younger children were gathering in the main cabin with expectant grins on their faces, waiting to see the dreaded operation commence.

"Bobby plugged the head so now he has to hold the bag while Daddy pumps up the pressure," announced 10-year old Devereau with authority.

"What will happen if it springs a leak?" asked Charmian, our 7-year old.

"It just means splat-splat all over the place!" proclaimed Devereau, who was always quick with graphic explanations for the benefit of his younger sister.

As if going to his execution, Bobby took the plastic bag from me, checked it for leaks and dutifully followed Charles to the forward head. There was silence in the main cabin as we strained our ears to hear any sounds from the action going on in the forward part of the boat. Nothing was heard but a few muted words of instruction followed by some muffled sounds and then Charles' cheerful voice saying,

"There you go, nothing to it. Up you go, empty it overboard and don't spill any on the way!"

With the arrogance wiped from his face Bobby returned to the main cabin and dolefully looked to his mother, "Believe me, Mom, I'm never going to use so much toilet paper again!"

Basket seller at Bahia Navidad

The 700-mile slog against headwinds and opposing seas was slow going and very tiring but we managed to arrive in San Diego by June 1, just when insurance coverage became void at the beginning of the hurricane season. While tied up at the marina we had left six months

125

previously, we were visited by some of the cruisers who had given us sketches of a few mainland anchorages. They were interested in whether we had managed to get to some of their favorite spots, and we were happy to share tales of our cruising experiences. Charles showed them the sketches he had drawn and they immediately suggested that he write an article to accompany the sketches and send it to *Cruising World* so other cruisers could have the benefit of his work. To our delight two groups of drawings and accompanying text were printed in the December, 1977 and January, 1978 editions of *Cruising World*.

We realized that Charles' health was not up to the demands of prolonged coastal cruising and decided that we must follow through on our decision to sell *Frodo* and return to life ashore. Once more, the less demanding cruising in the protected waters of the Pacific Northwest beckoned. We regretted having sold *Ern,* for she was the ideal size for us to enjoy trips with the family visiting the countless inlets and coves along the British Columbia coast.

"We should have put *Ern* on the hard and let her wait for us while we cruised in our Spencer 51."

"Yeah, but how were we to know how things would turn out?"

Regretting our actions couldn't turn back the clock.

The layout and quality workmanship we had put into the rigging and interior of *Frodo* had produced an ideal family cruising vessel. Within a few months our beautiful fiberglass vessel was sold to cruisers planning to travel to Polynesia, and *Frodo* completed our dream trip without us.

While waiting for *Frodo* to be sold, Charles began writing a book on construction details for the amateur boat builder. In addition, he wrote numerous technical articles that appeared in both *Sail* and *Cruising World*. Not to be outdone, I wrote three articles under a pseudonym, hoping that if my writing were to be published it would be on my own merit, not because I was tagging along with Charles E. Wood.

When we returned to British Columbia, Charles completed the book on boat building. Its printing was delayed and *Building Your Dream Boat* was eventually published by Cornell Maritime Press in 1981. We had hoped to earn a rewarding income from royalties, but special discounts to book clubs and distributors made for disappointing quarterly checks, a picayune return for the endless hours and energy he had put into its creation. Words from a fellow first-time author turned out to be prophetic: "Take it from me, unless you write about sin, sex, death or disaster, forget about making a buck on your first book, for all it amounts to is an ego trip."

Sailing along the east coast of Isla Espiritu Santo

11   *Ern* Returns

We returned to Vancouver at the end of the school year to pick up life ashore and intending at long last to build the boat Charles had designed many years ago. I returned to teaching in order to maintain a cash flow while our children resumed their education at a local school.

We had just settled into our new home when Fate stepped in with a timely, too-good-to-be-true incident. Charles glanced at the "Boats For Sale" section of the *Vancouver Sun* when suddenly he shouted out with a start, "Can you believe it, it sounds like *Ern* is for sale!" In a state of great excitement I dialed the number in the ad and trying not to sound too knowledgeable about boats, inquired about the beam, draft, engine and cabin layout. I repeated the answers to each question so Charles could get the information as soon as possible. When I asked about the vessel's name the reply was a rather hesitant,

"It seems to be Erin but it's spelled wrong, just E-R-N."

"When and where can we see her?"

"In Mosquito Creek Marina in North Vancouver."

"We know where it is. Will ten o'clock tomorrow be OK?"

Charles and I agreed on the offer to be made if she was still sound and decided how we would proceed to thoroughly check her over. We were like youngsters the day before Christmas as we eagerly awaited the next day.

What a thrill, to see the familiar lines of our old friend as she lay on the hard. After a brief conversation we learned that Don had purchased her in a state of sad disrepair and had commenced the time-consuming and money-eating process of refurbishing her only to find that his business demands left him with an insufficient amount of both ingredients. We asked what he knew about the previous owners and he replied,

"She was owned by some hippies, and before that an old couple sailed her in the Caribbean before bringing her to the west coast."

We managed to refrain from laughing as we realized that the "old couple" referred to was us.

"Good grief" we later chuckled, "If we were considered an 'Old Couple' when we were in our thirties what would we be considered now that we were in our forties?"

After giving her a thorough check-over Charles quietly told me to try to come to an agreement on price with Don, for he was satisfied that she was sound and regardless of the mast's condition, we should buy her. Then he strolled over to the shed where the mast was stored and left the horse-trading to me. My training in bargaining in Mexico rose to the occasion as I began to discuss price with the owner,

"She doesn't have an engine and there's a lot of work to be done bringing her up to scratch."

"But she's a sound boat and well built."

"I know that, but there's a lot of work to do and besides where's the engine?"

"It's a gas engine that needs some work. I'd rather keep it."

"Keep the engine, but that should bring your asking price down."

"All right, but that will drop it only $500, leaving us $750 apart."

We bargained back and forth for a few minutes until we were still $500 apart. Finally I remembered a dining room table and chairs that we had stored with friends during our cruise to Mexico.

"Could you use a beautiful, extra-wide extendable Danish modern teak dining room table with six high-back black, upholstered and very comfortable chairs? They cost well over $1,000 and are in excellent shape."

He looked at me strangely and replied,

"It's odd that you mentioned this as I was about to look for furniture for a small board room. Would this set be suitable?"

"It would be perfect, especially since the table can be extended at both ends," I enthusiastically assured him.

"Well, if the set is as you describe it then we've got a deal."

Just then Charles returned from the mast inspection and Don repeated, "You've just bought a boat if that dining set is as your wife described it."

Completely forgetting about the table and chairs Charles looked at him in amazement and replied with a perplexed look on his face,

"What table and chairs—what are you talking about?"

I nudged him rather firmly and said,

"Don't you remember the teak dining set we stored with friends when we went to Mexico?"

"Oh, of course, it just slipped my mind for a moment."

I couldn't blame Don as he suspiciously looked first at me and then at Charles.

"You're sure there really is a dining set? I think I'd better have a look at it before we go any further."

Within a few days the dining set passed his inspection, the balance was paid, and *Ern* became ours once again. We immediately had her hauled to our home where a cradle was constructed in a large shed. There was much work to do on her, for her exterior was badly weathered and needed many hours of scraping, sanding, varnishing and painting. A new engine and fuel tanks were installed, wiring and plumbing were replaced and the cockpit was rebuilt. All this took several years to accomplish, until she was ready to re-launch in 1981. In spite of Charles' health and our family obligations we continued to dream and plan for another extensive trip. Would we ever overcome the urge to sail and visit distant shores?

Launching Ern

12   *Charlie's Charts* is Born

During the time we were slowly bringing *Ern* back to life, we often received letters from cruisers who had seen a copy of Charles' articles and sketches of Mexican anchorages printed in *Cruising World*. They asked if Charles had drawings of other anchorages in Mexico and if so, how they could be obtained.

Eventually Harry Merrick, the publisher of *Baja Traveler*, an automobile and airplane guide to Mexico, offered Charles trips and flights over the coast if he would produce a boating section for his publication. He wanted photographs taken from the air with an overlay showing safe approaches to anchorages, following the same format used in his previous edition. Charles gladly accepted the offer and made several trips surveying and photographing anchorages in a single-engine plane with Monty Navarre, an accomplished bush pilot and photographer who regularly visited Baja. The slow, low-flying airplane provided an excellent opportunity to photograph anchorages where shoals, rocks and reefs could be easily identified.

Once the overlays were completed as requested, we concluded that Charles' hand-drawn sketches and sea-view profiles were more informative to a cruiser at sea level than photographs taken from the air with a bird's-eye view. Charles accordingly produced a complete set of hand-drawn sketches, and presented both sets to Mr. Merrick who chose the photographic version and returned the hand-drawn sketches as he had no use for them.

We felt that the hand-drawn sketches and land profiles had practical use for cruisers and that a guide devoted to cruising the western coast of Mexico would be a worthwhile venture, so we decided to publish one. First, we had to decide on a name. Charles wanted the no-nonsense title, "A Cruiser's Guide to Anchorages in Baja California and the Western Coast of Mexico." This I thought was too long and cumbersome. I suggested "Charlie's Charts of Western Mexico," which he disliked, for he cringed when people addressed his as "Charlie." He seemed to feel that this casual name was overly familiar and much preferred "Charles." The only other "Charlie" I had known was a draft horse, so I too was quite comfortable with his preference for the name "Charles." I asked one of my fellow teachers who had a quick wit what he thought of the titles we were considering. He agreed that Charles' suggestion was too long and also thought that my idea sounded rather casual though it might have some merit. Not hesitating for another moment he suggested, "Just call it 'Where the Baja Are We?'"

His suggestion was good for a laugh but we didn't want to imply that the guide was limited to Baja. Finally unable to think of anything better, we settled on the familiarity of "Charlie" and *Charlie's Charts* was born.

We didn't feel it was right to publish our guide quickly, since so much information had been obtained as a result of the trips Charles had with Harry Merrick and Monty Navarre. Thus we delayed making arrangements to print *Charlie's Charts of Mexico* for a year, hoping that the next edition of *Baja Traveler* would be published ahead of our home made guide. But the new edition of *Baja Traveler* was also delayed for various reasons, so we finally went ahead and investigated arrangements for printing the book.

Our finances were limited and we were uncertain as to how long it would take to recover our costs, so it was necessary to look for the most economical method of venturing out on this self-publishing limb. The graphic arts teacher at school offered to use the production of plates as an assignment for his class, provided that we paid for the materials. After investigating professional printing costs for a small run of 1,000 books we decided to follow up on the teacher's offer. More-over, his best senior student was looking for a summer job and jumped at the chance to print the book on a borrowed offset printer for the princely sum of $500.

Bound for Hawaii

During the summer, while the first edition of *Charlie's Charts of Mexico* was being printed, we sailed *Ern* to Hawaii. Although this was our first oceanic voyage, previous trips had been good preparation and we departed with no fanfare and in calm anticipation. Because of our doubts as to Charles' strength and endurance for the trip we took Bill, an experienced sailor, as crew.

A day after we left the mainland we were once again treated to a memorable sight when we were well offshore. Similar to the Isla Isabela experience in Mexico, the refracted light provided us with a sunrise in which the distant coastal mountains were featured quite clearly, yet when the sun rose higher in the sky they suddenly disappeared.

We had a few days of easy sailing but the weather did not cooperate. El Nino disrupted the normal wind patterns adjacent to the North Pacific High and as we approached the Hawaiian Islands, the far-flung effects of Hurricane Daniel resulted in only one day of recognizable trade winds. Much of the time we had weather typical of the doldrums: little or no wind, sloppy seas, cloudy skies and squalls.

Fair sailing

Throughout the voyage we were disturbed by the frequent sight of floating debris: beer cans, plastic containers and other trash. If there was this much rubbish on our single track across the ocean then the sum of all possible tracks must represent staggering amounts. I resolved to raise awareness of this travesty. Each *Charlie's Charts* published since then has contained a page on how debris harms marine life. In addition to the disappointment of seeing our once pristine Pacific sullied in this manner, our hopes for good sailing winds and respectable daily runs did not materialize.

135

A remnant of the days when *Ern* had been owned by hippies was a leaf-like pattern carefully carved on each of the large mahogany mainsheet cleats located aft of the cockpit. I had tried to sand them out but the carving was too deep and besides it made a rather attractive pattern in the wood. Some time into the trip Bill casually commented,

"I didn't think you were into smoking pot, Charles."

"What the hell are you talking about? Of course I don't," he retorted.

"Well what are the marijuana leaves carved in those cleats all about?"

"Gawd, are those marijuana leaves—I thought they were some kind of stylized conifer fronds! You've got to be kidding."

"Believe me that's what they are—I know them when I see them!"

"What will the Customs and the Agriculture Inspector do when we are inspected on entry? How can we hide them so they don't get suspicious?"

"We'll just have to leave a jacket casually thrown over one of them, and I can sit on the other," I suggested.

After 25 days of slow progress in frustrating conditions, we finally saw the illusive Mauna Kea volcano dimly outlined above the haze. As we approached the Big Island we were treated to the rich, fruity scent of lush greenery and sugar cane mills. To prepare for our inspection a jacket was casually draped over one of the telltale cleats. And when Hawaiian officialdom came aboard I remained awkwardly perched on top of an artistically carved cleat instead of sitting on comfortable, padded cockpit seats.

Our landfall was timely. Bill had to return to work on the mainland and we had made flight arrangements for Devereau and Charmian to join us in a couple of days. As jubilant as we were to have completed the crossing and reached our destination we were once again reminded

Chilkoot Pass summit on the Alaska/Yukon border

Tioman Island, Malaysia

West Coast Trail, Vancouver Island

Junkanoo parade in Nassau, Bahama Islands

Dugout in Rio Negro, near Manaus, Brazil

Mother and daughter in Grenada

View from "The Baths" on Virgin Gorda, Virgin Islands

Tea service, Beijing, China

The Summer Palace at Beijing, China

Puerto Viejo beach, Costa Rica

Stained glass walls of the Botanical Gardens, Toluca, Mexico

Tropical blossom, lion's paw (Heliconia Marginata)

Baie des Vierges, Fatu Hiva, Iles Marquises

The faces of Polynesia

Bald eagle in Tracy Arm, Alaska

Winter sunset, Tofino, Vancouver Island

that Charles did not have the strength and endurance needed for offshore passages. By the time we reached the Big Island his lack of energy made Charles irritable and difficult to live with. Our dream of sailing the Polynesian Islands, even in easy stages, was well and truly

City of Refuge, Island of Hawaii

finished. We took a brief cruise, then we returned to Vancouver by air after hiring crew to sail *Ern* back for us.

In Vancouver we were greeted with the good news that the printing of our cruising guide was complete. We took delivery of a truckload of 83 boxes of printed pages, lined the cartons up on the ping-pong table and on shelves in the recreation room, and optimistically hoped that our efforts would soon be rewarded. The painstaking task of collating each book by hand began. The children were commandeered to help with this tedious process. Even the promise of extra spending money was not enought to hold their interest and they soon complained that they'd rather go outside and play.

After a few books had been assembled I noticed that some of the pages had unsightly ink spatters, and that patches of faded printing made the text almost unreadable in places. What a tedious job—it was necessary to turn each page over to check that both sides were legible. before picking up the next page. I couldn't expect the children to make decisions about quality control, so I put the books together myself as a break from laundry, cooking, teaching school and trying to be a Mom. Charles, wanting to have some mental stimulation, turned his attention to the formation of a private engineering firm, that eventually became the holding company for *Charlie's Charts*.

We placed advertisements in yachting magazines and waited for the orders to start coming in. We waited and we waited, and finally after a month we received one lonely order in the mail! The piles of assembled books seemed to mock us.

"With 1,000 books to sell we could be giving a Christmas present of *Charlie's Charts to Mexico* to 100 friends for 10 years or to 10 friends for 100 years!"

"But we don't have 100 friends who want to cruise to Mexico— besides no one wants 10 copies of the same book. We won't have any friends left if we start unloading unwanted cruising guides on them."

"What are we going to do with them? Surely someone will buy the book if we can get it into a bookstore where advertising-resistant cruisers can see it."

Since it was necessary for Charles to meet some engineering associates in San Diego he took along 12 guides in the hope of selling them to marine chart dealers. Two of the stores he visited each took three copies and one store took six copies. He returned home triumphant from his first and only book-selling trip. Within a few days the telephone was ringing with wild abandon as news spread among cruisers. Orders started coming in from stores all along the Pacific coast as well as Florida and the east coast. We had estimated that 1,000 copies would take two or three years to sell but to our surprise the entire supply was sold in less than a year. *Charlie's Charts* had arrived!

Buoyed up by the success of the Mexican guide Charles then flew to Polynesia the following year where he joined cruising friends and chartered boats to visit various islands to obtain material for a guide to Polynesia. Shortly thereafter he took several trips visiting ports and anchorages of the Hawaiian Islands and we produced a guide covering that area also.

I continued to teach, act as the salesman, shipper and accountant for *Charlie's Charts* and care for our children. Feeling that I was missing out on the action, I suggested that we cruise to Alaska and prepare a guide covering a route following the coast of British Columbia and the Inside Passage to Glacier Bay.

"Nonsense, no one wants to cruise to Alaska."

"But there's such great scenery on the British Columbia coast and besides I'd like to do some cruising—you've been getting all the trips."

"Forget it, it's a bad idea."

Some time later Frank, the manager of *Captain's Nautical Supply* marine store in Portland, asked when I was delivering some books,

"Why don't you guys do a guide to Alaska? A lot of people have been asking if such a book exists." Bounding to the car I relayed the suggestion to Charles and his response was predictable,

"Hey, that sounds like a great idea—we could easily make the trip during the summer holidays and you could come along."

How typical of a man: a suggestion from his wife had no logic but if a guy made the same suggestion then it probably had a lot of merit. Trying not to remind him that it was my idea in the first place, I cheerfully helped to start planning for a cruise to Alaska the following year.

13   North to Alaska

How ironic—until this trip our cruises had been focused on going far afield to warmer climes where images of white sand beaches and blue-green waters caught our attention, yet here on our doorstep we were blessed with one of the greatest and most scenic cruising areas of the world. In the 700 miles of linear distance the coastline measures over 25,000 miles—more than the circumference of the earth! While examining hydrographic charts and reading the Sailing Directions we soon began to appreciate the infinite number of inlets, bays and coves that provide excellent anchorages on the proposed route.

We planned that Charles would take four weeks to travel to Juneau, Alaska where I would join him at the end of the school year for the return trip. He would have preferred to have single-handed on the northbound part of the trip but we both realized that, given the uncertain state of his health, taking a one-man crew would be safer. And so Charles and Harry, an acquaintance, set off in the latter part of May.

Though they complained about the cold temperatures, their description of the scenery was generously sprinkled with superlatives and the photographs taken were proof of spectacular sights. The snowfall had been heavy the previous winter and the mountains were streaked with cascades of run-off hurtling down the steep rocky faces.

Surprisingly, in spite of the prevailing northwesterlies, they had many days of favorable winds for sailing on the northbound trip.

Conning a route through bergie bits

At the end of the school year I flew to Juneau, and joined the twosome one cold and windy day. I had left the warmth of a minor heat wave in Vancouver, and was quite taken aback by the cold wind and near freezing temperature as I stepped off the plane. But once aboard our cozy boat with the warmth of the stove and glow of the kerosene lamps I was right back at home again, glad to be aboard.

"It's like taking a boat trip to the Himalayas."

"Breathtaking."

"Fabulous."

"Magnificent."

"There simply isn't a word strong enough to express how I feel."

The emerging view of the Fairweather Range in Glacier Bay was a wonderful reward for the effort made to visit the area. The snow-covered peaks towered above glaciers as they crept down to the water's edge; we had the best of both worlds, spectacular alpine scenery surrounded us as we cruised in our own familiar *Ern*.

One crisp, calm morning we experienced a dramatic series of mirages as we traveled in Glacier Bay. Suddenly towers of icy pillars appeared some distance ahead of us, only to disappear just as quickly. Minutes later an islet in the distance would appear to be actually inverted, but a glance back in a few moments and it had resumed its normal shape. Beautiful. We set up our headquarters in Blue Mouse Cove and reveled in the days spent exploring Glacier Bay and later the narrower, less-traveled Muir Inlet.

The distance traveled by glaciers varies from year to year. This year small craft were unable to get near to the face of glaciers in the northernmost part of the bay. However, we were able to approach Reid Glacier with no difficulty, and anchored *Ern* about a quarter of a mile from the face of the glacier so she would be in no danger if a towering block of ice calved (broke off) from its seaward edge. Where we were anchored, sharp waves that may have been created from such an occurrence would have been just a slight swell by the time they reached *Ern*. We launched *Angus*, the inflatable, approached the head of the bay, dodged some bergy bits scattered about and went ashore a short distance from the glacier. Charles was the last person to disembark so he tied *Angus* to a rock and proceeded to photograph tiny pink flowers bravely growing in the harsh environment.

Harry and I scrambled over a few sharp boulders until we reached the moraine left from the receding glacier: a mixture of gravel, rocks and coarse sand where there was a faint trail. After climbing a knoll and descending the far side Charles and *Angus* were no longer visible. From a distance the full impact of the glacier size could not be appreciated. But as we approached the dirt-speckled, bluish-white broken towers of compressed snow, the immensity of the river of ice became apparent. It was so spectacular that I went back to get Charles and the camera, as I felt that excellent photographs could be taken here.

We walked slowly, gazing at the beautiful scenery and approached the glacier. Charles wanted to get some perspective in the photographs, and asked me to move to a spot that seemed awfully close to the towers of ice at its edge.

"Hurry up and take the picture, I want to get away from here!"

"Just one more, now move back just a little."

"Are you finished? Hurry up!"

Reid Glacier in Glacier Bay

I began to get anxious. The grinding, crunching, squeaking sounds generated by the slow movement of the tons of ice creeping towards the sea had an ominous message and I was extremely intimidated. Glancing at the massive blocks of ice high above me I wondered

143

how long it would be before they broke loose and tumbled down with a roar. I picked out an escape route to use the instant the glacier gave any sign of calving, but fortunately it wasn't necessary to follow my plan of action. I was greatly relieved when the photography was complete and I was able to withdraw to a safe distance before we hiked back to the inflatable.

Rounding the last corner we were faced with an unbelievable sight. During the hour or so we had been ashore the tide had risen so much that *Angus* was afloat about 50 feet from shore, still tied securely to a rock. There were no other boats in sight that could help us out of our predicament so there was no alternative but for one of us to wade into the icy water to retrieve the inflatable.

"I'll go for it, Charles. You shouldn't be putting your body into that icy water," I said.

"No, it's my fault for not hauling it up further. I knew that the tidal range in these higher latitudes was greater than down south but I forgot to take it into consideration when I hauled *Angus* on shore. I blew it."

"Remember, you did have a heart attack and this is the last thing your body needs," I argued.

"Listen, since we started boating we've had a rule that whoever messes up around the boat is the one who'll have to fix it up. I messed up so I'll go in and get the damn thing."

He was absolutely adamant and I knew there was no point in arguing, so I quietly took his clothes as he stripped down to all but his undershirt and sea boots. Harry and I watched in silence as he slowly made his way into the icy water and cautiously groped his way toward *Angus*. It was a tense and troubling few minutes, for the sudden jolt of immersion in near freezing water could have put his body into shock. He was not the strong, intrepid mountaineer I had married and his general health, though not fragile, was certainly vulnerable.

By the time he reached *Angus,* the icy water was above his waist. He vigorously yanked on the painter tied to the rock but it held firm. He took a deep breath and heaved on the line with an even greater pull.

Brr!

It came free and Harry and I let out a cheer. Charles gave a sigh and slowly hauled *Angus* back to shore. We immediately began to give our shivering captain a brisk rubdown to dry his whitened skin and encourage blood circulation.

"It's so cold I was numb from the waist down, with the only fear I had being that I didn't want to immerse my head in the water—it was the only part of me that felt warm," he chattered.

Glancing down as we continued to dry him off, I had to stifle a laugh that was hard to control after the desperate tension of the past few minutes.

"What are you laughing about?" he snapped at me.

The suppressed giggles began to surface and I was hard pressed to speak clearly. "Honey, when you went into the water you were a guy, but now that you're out you've turned into a girl!"

We all looked down at where his manly attributes once were and there was nothing. Simultaneously the three of us burst out laughing and the tension suddenly disappeared. It was a relief to hear his hearty laugh and know that his sense of humor had remained intact.

After we returned to *Ern* he drank two mugs of hot, sweet lemonade, changed to dry clothing and soon recovered from the ordeal, thankfully with no lasting ill effects.

In the ice pack before Muir Glacier

Our visit to Muir Inlet was like entering another world as its narrow confines prohibited entry to cruise ships and charter boats. The sounds of these large vessels crashing through patches of bergy bits in Glacier Bay were here replaced by the cries of newborn seals calling for their mothers. Because the walls of Muir Inlet have more recently been scoured by glacial action there is a paucity of growth clinging to the rocky surfaces, giving it a newly scrubbed and pristine appearance.

We tried to approach McBride Glacier but we were forced to abandon the attempt because the water was congested with bergy bits of every size and shape. The constant crunch of ice bumping into the hull was nerve-wracking, but try as we might with careful conning it was impossible to progress without feeling under attack. Though fascinated by the constant lazy circling movement of the ice, I was very relieved when Charles decided to leave the clogged inlet and turn our bow southward.

Daily sightings of wildlife added much interest to our travel along the coast. Bald eagles soaring in solitude provided just as much interest as a flock of over 30 seen on one beach in an area known for prolific marine life. Humpback, finback and gray whales, sea otters floating on the water as they munched on sea urchins and the moving white specks of mountain goats high in the mountains were a constant source of wonder.

Seal pups on the ice-floes of Muir Inlet

Our stopover in Sitka proved to be an educational experience. In addition to its Russian past and American present, the British flag has also flown over the area. What caught my attention was that in spite of the cold war and its aftermath, Russian artifacts and culture were given top billing in museums and gift shops. At a time when anything Russian was viewed negatively in the lower 48 states, here, in Sitka the welcoming ceremony for cruise ships included a bevy of young girls in Russian costumes dancing Russian folk dances.

Within a month, we arrived back in our slip in Vancouver with reams of information, several hundred slides, numerous sketches and a host of memories from a successful voyage. We realized that we had only skimmed the surface of the hundreds of inlets and coves that dot the coast and that many cruises to the north could be taken without repeat visits to many anchorages. We resolved that in the future we would head north to the Queen Charlotte Islands, circumnavigate Vancouver Island and visit the countless remote inlets along the coast of this wildly beautiful province.

It took a year for Charles to assemble the material collected on our Alaskan cruise, complete the sketched charts, draw finished copies of the rough sketches of land profiles and compose the text. I typed the various drafts in my spare time after school and continued to market the other guides. Our only hesitation in producing *Charlie's Charts North to Alaska* was our contributing to the loss of the area's charms — its isolation and lack of congestion. However, by this time the cruising population of North America was expanding and boaters were determined to explore this coast, so invasion of the region seemed inevitable.

14 Sinking and Salvage

"*When are you going to produce a guide that takes us safely along the west coast of the United States? Once we enter Mexico, Polynesia or British Columbia you take us by the hand and give us practical advice, but to get to the starting point we have to travel north or south along the Washington to California coast and we need your help.*"

This part of a letter echoed comments from a number of cruisers, and prompted us to commence work on a guide to the west coast of the United States. After we had published *Charlie's Charts North to Alaska* there was a geographic gap in our publications and it seemed logical to correct this omission. We were aware that this section of coast could not be considered a cruising destination, but since it covered a significant distance that must be passed in order to reach areas north or south of Continental United States, we felt that it was a legitimate addition to our guides.

Charles and I worked well as a team and had developed an efficient system that suited our individual strengths. We had sailed along the coast on previous occasions, but now detailed information on ports and harbors was needed to provide substance to the text. The quickest means of collecting shore-based material was by car, and time was a factor to consider as I continued to teach while the children completed high school. From the Pacific Northwest we drove as far south as Santa Barbara during summer vacation, stopping at every harbor along the coast.

We planned to visit the remaining part of southern California during the upcoming Christmas vacation. Charles sketched each harbor plan while I collected information on the location of marine supplies, grocery stores, restaurants, the Coast Guard station and sources of propane, fuel, kerosene and other items important to a cruiser. We discovered many unique points of interest in the small coastal towns we had not visited previously during our many trips along the coast either by car or boat.

Upon returning to Vancouver Charles began drawing the detailed plans of harbor facilities and incorporated the collateral material I had researched. He completed the sketches of ports and marinas from Anacortes to the location chart for Santa Cruz and he began to write the first few pages of the introduction. Not satisfied with his first four drafts, he wrote a fifth and final version, and laid it neatly on his desk beside the stack of hand-drawn charts.

Driftwood on a Washington beach

"An ambulance has just arrived at the hospital with your husband. Can you come in as soon as possible?"

"Yes, I'll be there in about half an hour."

The terse voice on the telephone relayed a message I had been dreading for 13 years, ever since his first heart attack. Deliberately driving at less than the speed limit I told myself I had to accept the reality of his collapse, which had occurred just a few minutes after I had left for school. In my heart I knew that our life together was about to end. I made a point of breathing deeply and evenly as I'd practiced in Yoga classes. I did not cry.

The agony and turmoil of the 10-day period that elapsed until Charles passed away was hell. Though I made a gallant effort to return to school following the memorial service it was no use, and after a traumatic week I took a leave of absence hoping that in a few months, I could pick up the threads of my former life and finish the school year. But this was not a realistic solution. Some time later I resigned from teaching permanently.

It was autumn. I welcomed the sanctuary of our home with its long tree-lined driveway. The task of raking up fall leaves and cedar twigs scattered on the lawn was timely and somewhat therapeutic. As if trying to sweep away the shock of his loss I viciously piled up the once bright colors, now faded into ochre and dull brown shades. But like the approaching winter that had to be endured before the fresh leaves of a new year burst forth, I had to pass through a dormant time. A black, windowless room seemed to surround me, obliterating any thoughts of the future. I felt as if there was no escape, not even a tiny gap in the nothingness.

I was angry that one who was so bright and accomplished could be taken so quickly when there was still much he had left to do. One day I was lined up in a short queue at the bank. A small, slightly stooped, elderly lady in a gray coat topped with a frumpy faded green hat was leaning over the counter straining to hear the teller.

"What's that yer saying, I can't hear you," she croaked. "Say it again."

I couldn't bear to stay any longer. I had the dreadful urge to push my way through the line, rush over and shake her. I just wanted to scream.

"Why, for God's sake, why are you still alive and my husband is dead?"

I fled from the bank. I was close to losing it. I drove home and started to rake leaves again.

Though I was weary and depleted, sleep would not rescue me from my cold reality. Night after night I'd toss and turn until the wee hours of the morning when I'd finally fall into a restless sleep. When morning came my jaws were set firm from grinding my teeth so hard that several fillings had to be replaced with crowns. For a time I shunned my friends, for I wanted only to talk about Charles and the life we had enjoyed together, but they would change the subject and try to interest me in current events or the stock market or other "diversions" from my pain. Fortunately, there were three friends who understood, as they had also suffered the loss of a loved one. We opened our hearts and souls to each other and healing, though infinitesimally slow, eventually came.

Like an automaton, I went about the process of shipping guides to retailers and the routine provided something for me to hang on to from the past. I pored over the neat pile of sketched drawings Charles had been working on, topped with an unfinished detail of the harbor at Santa Cruz. I was determined not to discard the results of the hours of work Charles had put into those pages, especially since he had often said this guide would be even better than the preceeding ones.

I made a photocopy of his unfinished sketch and started trying to print the labels. What an unsightly mess—some printing went below the line, some above, some letters were clearly a different size than the ones before or slanted, and all were poorly formed; even the letter "l" was shaky. After smudging the final label I left in disgust and went outside to rake more leaves.

After the usual sleepless night I made another photocopy and tried once more to complete the labeling and some dock details. This time there was a slight improvement over the previous day's effort, but as I reviewed my work my hand shook and some coffee dripped on the page, ruining it. Back to the leaves . . .

By the end of the third day a few labels appeared to be the best ones yet, but I realized that the task of printing small letters uniformly on a complete sketch was clearly beyond me. Cutting and pasting the best part of all three pages together I made a photocopy of my three days of hard work. When Charmian came home from work at the end of the day I showed her the results of my efforts. She looked at them for a few minutes then a pinched crease formed at the corners of her mouth as she quietly said,

"Mom, don't you think you'd better get someone else to do the charts?"

She couldn't have said it better. Looking back at the page I saw it for what it was—a dreadful mess. I contacted several people who agreed to reproduce harbor and dock plans and print the labels that were needed. One of these was Richard Miller, a university student who generously completed the remaining charts. His ability as an illustrator made a valuable contribution to subsequent editions in beautiful drawings that are a worthwhile tool for identification of different marine animals.

The next big task to be tackled was to compose the text accompanying the sketches. For the book to have credibility I felt that it needed a person who was respected in cruising circles to finish the work Charles had started. With this in mind, I contacted John Guzzwell, the well known sailor, boatbuilder and author of *Trekka Round the World*. We met in a little coffee shop near Seattle's Lake Union and after a brief time recalling the occasion when we met many years ago following his trip around the world, I asked if he would be willing to do the job.

"Oh no, I'm right in the middle of building a research vessel for the University of Hawaii and it's just about to be launched. I'm sorry but I just haven't got the time."

My heart fell and I slumped in the seat, disappointment showing on my face.

"Can you suggest anyone else who might be able to do the job?"

"Well, Margo," he quietly replied, "Why don't you do it? You know Charles' pattern and the kind of information he would write."

"Me do it? Me?" My ability to speak proper English failed.

"Of course you can, you can do it, I'm sure you can!"

With such an unexpected endorsement coming from someone like John Guzzwell I felt my back straighten up and I began to sit a little more erect.

"I'd never dreamed of writing the text, but maybe I could

154

give it a try."

"Of course you should."

When I drove home my mind was a-buzz with the prospect of taking on the job of writing material for the book. Clearly, I was unable to do an acceptable job of printing on the charts but maybe, just maybe, I could make a go of writing. But one gnawing thought gave me concern, for long ago my school marks in English had not matched those attained in other subjects. I began to regret not having put forth a better effort. I'd just have to find a good editor.

The next day I sat down and wrote several paragraphs describing one of the simpler entrances to Anacortes, Washington. On reading my effort the following morning I realized it was disorganized and turgid. Taking a clean sheet of paper I wrote another description of the same harbor. A day later my rereading session ended in disgust as I said aloud,

"Charles, if you had written something as disorganized as this, I wouldn't have typed it."

A little voice inside me said, *"Smarten up, look for a pattern in the way he wrote a description and follow it; don't try to start from zero and develop your own style."*

After reading his description of several harbors in other guides I recognized a simple pattern to the way he described the approach to an area, whether it was an anchorage or a town with marina facilities. After making a template of topics to be covered I then wrote a description following the model. Day four arrived and when I read my last attempt at a write-up I felt a surge of pride, for at last I had written something that followed a logical format.

Days passed and each one found me polishing the work from the previous week before writing material for the next harbor. By January the text and sketches were complete except for the Los Angeles to San Diego section. I had to make the trip alone that we had planned for the

Christmas school vacation. I armed myself with as much material as I could find from charts and sailing magazines and flew to San Diego, rented a car and from there drove to Los Angeles, visiting the major marinas along the coast.

I hated going to restaurants, for the hostess would invariably greet me with a forced smile and finding that I was alone would say in a loud voice, "Just a table for ONE?" They could see that I was alone and carrying a sheaf of papers so I had something to look at while waiting to be served so why did they have to say "one" so loudly? I was still very fragile and sensitive, but I was beginning to move on. At home, the leaves had been raked up and only the bare, cold ground remained.

Monterey Cypress on the 17-mile drive

During sales trips in the past Charles had driven the car while I navigated as we traversed greater Los Angeles, using various freeways. But now I was alone and had to do both jobs, so I carefully prepared for the challenging operation. Each morning I would make a list of the freeways to be followed and the exits and streets to be taken to arrive at each of the marinas I needed to visit. With the list propped on my lap I would set out with dogged determination. When about to leave *Ship's Store* in Marina del Rey I asked a young salesman for some advice on choice of freeways to be taken.

"Oh migawd, you won't find me driving on a freeway—they're too wild and dangerous!"

His reply gave me a jolt, for if a local Californian was too intimidated to drive the freeways, what was a little gray-haired old lady from Vancouver doing on the road? However, I got back in the car, braced myself and headed back to Interstate 405 and on to the next marina.

I had a lot of time for thought and planning while I was alone in the hotel at night. The problem of what to do about *Ern* often came to mind, until one night I made two lists, one titled "Reasons for Selling," the other, "Reasons for Keeping." The "Reasons for Selling" was the longer list so it made my decision. After returning home I had an appointment with the family doctor who had known us for many years.

"How are things going, Margo?" he asked.

"Oh, not bad. I just got back from LA and am busy finishing the US guide. I had time to sort out a few things and have decided to sell the boat."

"I usually don't tell people what to do in their private life but I'm telling you now, don't sell *Ern*. Even if she sits at the dock all summer, let her wait for at least a year before you decide to sell her. Don't do it now."

As I drove home his words echoed in my mind and I pondered his advice. Then another thought entered my head: '*What kind of a wimp am I if I let a beautiful boat like Ern sit at the dock all summer?*' So far each visit to the boat to check her winter cover had ended with my bursting into tears, for she was a visible reminder of the good trips we'd taken, the places we'd visited and the fact that trips we'd planned would never come to be. But now, with new determination, I looked at her differently. We would still go places. We would still have good trips. However, if I was now to be captain, I had new responsibilities, new lessons to learn. I looked at the engine and realized that this was my nemesis. I knew how to start it, put it into gear, speed up, slow down and stop but I didn't know how to maintain it, for Charles had looked after that. I had never docked the boat or taken her out of the slip—I'd always been the deck crew, waiting to give assistance as needed. There was too much that I didn't know about maintaining or operating the boat.

"Well, I'll just have to learn!" I said aloud to myself.

It took about two months to assemble the material collected in southern California and oversee the completion of the accompanying charts. During this period I registered for a course in diesel mechanics offered at a local night school.

"You've come to the wrong door," the redheaded instructor, young enough to be my son, greeted me as I approached the designated room.

"Isn't this Room 16?" I asked, wondering if the room numbers had been changed.

"Yes, but this is for Diesel Mechanics, you must be mistaken."

"I registered and paid the fees, could you check the list for my name, Wood?"

"Oh, so you're M. Wood," he said, looking at me in disbelief as he moved aside to let me pass through the doorway.

I walked into the class and was met by the stares of the all-male class: burly heavy-duty mechanics, ruddy-faced farmers, ranchers and truck drivers. It reminded me of the days when, as the only Protestant in a Catholic school I was a distinct and easily identifiable minority of one. However, determined not to be daunted, I attended classes regularly and though I didn't learn a great deal that was applicable to basic engine maintenance, the course gave me a wee bit of confidence and improved my attitude towards the engine. My status as an anomaly in the class remained to the end, for after each topic had been discussed the instructor would ask,

"Now class, are there any questions regarding this topic?"

Then, as if to underline the fact that there was a class and then there was Mrs. Wood, he would add,

"And Mrs. Wood, do you have any questions?"

When the diesel engine class was finished I signed up for a course in Electricity and Electronic Instrumentation thinking that I would gain a better understanding of another area of boating that Charles had been responsible for and of which I was ignorant. But shortly into the second class the course focused on television repair and I withdrew as it was of no interest to me.

As the weeks wore on I carried out a rigid discipline as I continued to write. Each day would start with reading and modifying the write-ups from the previous two days, followed by assembling the material and composing the text for the next harbor. Finally, the text completed, I sent several pages to the school where I had taught, asking one of the English teachers to give me some pointers for improving sentence structure and punctuation. To my dismay the pages were returned a few days later with the abrupt comment, "Why don't you just present your thoughts in point form and forget about writing sentences?"

These were harsh words but I knew my efforts couldn't be completely useless so I asked Helen, a good friend who was an elementary school teacher, if she would give me a few pointers. She came over and started to read the first page. Helen kept reading and without looking away from the page she leaned over, opened her purse, took out a red pencil and began to insert the odd comma, delete another and cross out unnecessary words. "This is fun," she said with a big smile on her face. "Actually, my degree is in English Literature and this is right up my alley. I've never thought of becoming an editor but yes, I'd be glad to edit the book for you." What a relief to know that my efforts could be salvaged! Within a few weeks editing was completed, the text was retyped and the book sent to the printers. As a reward for finishing the job that Charles and I had started, I took a cruise to the Amazon . . . but that's another story.

At work

An interesting peek at human nature presented itself in the midst of my grief. Less than a month after Charles' passing a letter came from a publisher of a Mexican guide that showed just how insensitive opportunists can be. Though the letter made me angry, more than that it made me determined to carry on *Charlie's Charts* with all the strength and determination I could muster. The letter read,

"I suppose now that Charles is dead you won't know what to do with the business so I'd like to get the right to print some of the sketches from the Mexican guide. The pages I want are as follows.......Oh yes, I will give some credit for the source of these drawings and will give you a reduced rate for advertising in our publication."

The writer ignored my refusal to dole out selected pages at random and sent a second letter. My final response was blunt and one that even he understood. This was fair warning to me that vultures were alive and well in the publishing industry.

Similarly, some years later a representative of a distributor, in the hopes of discrediting me and bolstering his sales of alternate guides, announced to several retailers that *Charlie's Charts* was no longer in business. His underhanded methods backfired and once more I worked even harder not to be bowled over by my male competitors.

15 Starting To Cruise Without My Captain

This was the day I had been bracing myself for since that provocative conversation with my doctor. I was going to move *Ern* by myself. I had spent a lot of time thinking about steps to be taken and the sequence that ought to be followed when moving her. What else was there to do? What had Charles done while I was busying myself stowing gear and readying the lines? For years I had thought of ways he could do a better job maneuvering the boat when we entered or left the dock. It seemed that often I was either making an Olympian leap to take a line ashore or I was heaving with all my strength to keep from bashing the dock, and of course I was regularly criticized for not doing the right thing. *Why doesn't he approach a little slower? Why does he come in at such a sharp angle? Why . . . why . . .* As I drove to the marina I rehearsed for one last time what had to be done and how I would make the 90° turn in confined space and then reverse *Ern* to enter the opening where the Travelift was located.

"I'll be over at the Travelift in about 10 minutes," I bravely said to the marina manager.

"Do you want a hand?"

"No, I'll be all right, thanks."

The engine started without any hesitation and my confidence rose. It sounded good and reminded me of other times when a great day's trip had begun with the comforting purr of the Volvo. I slowly maneuvered *Ern* into position, put the engine in reverse and backed her into the bay.

"Great job, better than all the yelling that goes on when we have a couple of macho guys bringing a boat in for the first time," said the lift operator.

"I guess I was a bit lucky," I replied, trying not to sound surprised.

Ern was gently lifted from the water and blocked up in a metal cradle. Whew! The first hurdle had been overcome and I felt a surge of satisfaction as I scrubbed the mud and slime from her hull and prepared her for painting. After her bottom and topsides had been painted and a fresh coat of varnish applied to her exterior woodwork I was filled with pride as *Ern* stood out from other vessels on the dock that had not had their spring brush-up.

All spruced up

Now I wanted to share the pleasure of sailing with friends who had been particularly kind to me following Charles' death so I invited three different families to join me for a day sail in the bay on successive weekends. Each time I went to the boat early, rigged the sails, wiped the cockpit and stowed lunch and drinks for the guests. My friends were enthusiastic about the experience and visit during the outing but to my chagrin, the typical response from the disappearing guests after a pleasant day on the water was,

"Thanks a lot for the sail, Margo. We've got to rush. It's been great—see you later!"

Since my guests were unfamiliar with the boat they were reticent to do anything while we were underway, but my generosity was stretched to the limit when their vanishing act occurred as soon as we returned to the dock. After each outing I cleaned up the cabin, picked up the odd forgotten toy, covered the mainsail, stowed the foresails, and rigged the cockpit cover. These easy tasks could have been done quickly with assistance, and the effort would have shown that my friends had appreciated the outing.

While thinking about what had happened during the outings with friends I reassessed the situation. *I love to be around the boat and cruise to new anchorages. Is it possible for me to regain these pleasures? If I were 30 years younger and 40 pounds lighter then perhaps someone would take me for a cruise, but who is going to invite a woman of my age? No one! Taking friends for a one-day sail leaves me feeling put-upon and besides, I'd like to cruise for at least a week or two. There's only one solution: it's a wild idea but I'll just have to try single-handing!*

Armed with these thoughts I invited one last couple out for a sail.

"Would you like to come for a sail and not do anything? I want to see if I can handle the boat by myself. If I need help, I'll call on you."

"We don't know what to do anyway, so that sounds great," was the reply. And so it was that my dry run at single-handing went without a hitch, and I felt that I was ready to try a trip on my own.

I told Devereau of my plan to single-hand on a short cruise and he replied, "Go ahead, Mom, you've done plenty of cruising, you know what to do." But when I told Charmian of my plan to sail to Desolation Sound alone she objected strongly, and pleaded with me to take a girlfriend along for company in case "something happens." Giving in to her concerns, I invited three girlfriends in succession for a one-week cruise to this beautiful area with its snug, protected anchorages.

Initially, each one accepted with enthusiasm but a few days later phoned me to decline the invitation with flimsy excuses ranging from

"I have to paper the spare bedroom for a house guest arriving next month."

"I think I should stay at home and do some gardening." Eventually, they each admitted to having cold feet about cruising with a woman, but if the same invitation had come from a man, they would have happily gone along. So much for women's lib!

I expected to depart on my first trip alone with butterflies in my stomach, but to my surprise I felt a calm eagerness. I was confident and determined to prove I could manage on my own with my old friend, *Ern*. I had taken a course offered by the U.S. Power Squadron , "Piloting, Seamanship and Small Boat Handling" while we were waiting for *Frodo* to be sold in San Diego. With that learning experience combined with practical knowledge gained from cruising, I felt that I was capable of navigating and safely handling the boat on a short trip along the coast. Unfortunately, I had been prohibited from taking the course that followed since at that time a woman was not permitted to enroll unless accompanied by a male partner.* *Charles, how I wish you'd joined me then, even though the course was redundant for you.*

This regulation is no longer in effect since a law suit in 1988 ruled that it was discriminatory.

As I looked across Semiahmoo Bay to Point Roberts, I began to enjoy my new found freedom and was happy I could do as I pleased without anyone to worry about, backseat drive, or criticize. It was a wonderful feeling of freedom, though somewhat bittersweet under the circumstances.

After I had rounded the buoy at Point Roberts and entered the Strait of Georgia the calm day dictated use of the motor. An hour or so later, a nice breeze came up and I was able to set the sails and move along nicely. A frequent difference of opinion between Charles and me had been whether to sail or use the motor. He preferred motoring unless the wind velocity would move the boat at 5 or 6 knots, whereas I preferred to sail if we could move along even at a slightly slower rate. He reasoned that night entrances should be avoided at all cost. Now at last I had the freedom to sail—and sail I did, tacking back and forth across the Strait and reveling in the sparkling sea and dancing bow wave.

"There, Charles, we can have a great sail without putting on the engine all the time," I said aloud, "This is the way it should be."

My destination: Keats Island Marine Park

A few hours later I glanced at the distant horizon and then at my watch and realized that it was already mid-afternoon and although I'd happily tacked back and forth across the Strait of Georgia, little progress had been made toward my destination because of the outgoing tide. The wind switched and began to come from dead ahead. I started the motor but to my chagrin now the temperature gauge and the tachometer had stopped working. I was forced to adjust the speed to what seemed like the right sound of the engine. *Charles, you could have made repairs in a couple of minutes, I'm so sorry I didn't pay more attention to what you were doing when you were working on the engine.*

The ebbing tide, combined with rising head seas slowed progress over the ground. To avoid making a night entrance at Gibsons I increased the speed several times, yet still progress seemed slow. I smelled smoke, opened a cockpit locker and to my dismay saw a cardboard box of engine supplies rimmed with red coals about to burst into flames. With the heeling of the boat the box had slid over and touched a spot on the exhaust pipe where there was a small gap in the insulation. I frantically pulled the box into the cockpit, brushed off the smoldering embers and doused the container. My heart thumped, and I shuddered at the thought of how close I'd been to disaster.

I was still miles from the entrance, and the night was fast approaching. *Oh well, I'll have to go to the marina rather than anchor.* A little powerboat streaked past me and its small running lights disappeared as it rounded the corner in the distance. By the time I entered the channel on this moonless night, darkness had fallen. I proceeded cautiously until breakwater lights showed the entrance to the basin. It was too late to arrange for moorage, so I tied to the fuel dock where years ago the operator had kindly let us stay for the night.

I was mentally and physically exhausted from the long day, shaken by my close call with fire and my first entrance alone at night. *Charles, are you laughing at me now?* I collapsed on the bunk and trembled as I tried to relax. Suddenly, a loud voice accompanied by a sharp snapping sound on the foredeck brought me to my feet. Then the sound was repeated on the deck over my head. I flung open the hatch and saw a gangly six-foot man carrying a double-bladed ax.

"What are you doing? I shouted as he untied my stern line and flung it over the lifelines, setting *Ern* adrift.

"What the hell are you doing on my dock? You yachtsmen think you can just tie up anywhere—get the hell away."

He then started to untie the mooring lines of the motorboat moored astern of me, while yelling the same message to its startled owners. There was no alternative but to move both boats to empty slips in the marina, hoping that long-term tenants would not return from late-night fishing trips and give us another tongue-lashing. What a way to start my single-handed adventure! *Maybe, Charles, just maybe I should have foregone that lovely sail and motored all the way. You were probably right, this time.*

A bright sun and blue skies greeted me the next morning, setting an optimistic tone for the day. My ESP didn't kick in and I suspected nothing of what the day held in store. I settled the moorage fee at the marina and made arrangements for a mechanic to drop down to the boat during the noon hour to repair the tachometer and temperature gauge. The only "pay" that was suggested was a "drop of whiskey." I tidied up the boat and eagerly awaited the arrival of the mechanic so that repairs could be completed and I could proceed to Smuggler Cove, the next anchorage, only a few miles distant.

"Here's Hank, that good mechanic I promised," a friendly voice called out.

"Come aboard, I just need repairs to the tachometer and temperature gauge—they just died on me a couple of hours after I got going yesterday."

Ern heeled slightly as the 250-pound, 6'6" mechanic lumbered aboard with a grunt. His two-day beard, rheumy eyes and disheveled greasy hair reminded me of a bloated Bill Sykes. *Thank goodness it shouldn't take long, this guy looks spooky.* Taking only a few minutes to make the necessary repairs he then lounged back on the bunk.

"Where's that drink I was promised?"

I put a bottle of Scotch on the table and poured a fair-sized drink that he gulped down as if it was water.

"Are you alone on the boat?"

"Yes, my husband passed away and I'm taking a trip along the coast."

"Well, that's something, running the boat yerself."

He poured a second tall drink, gazed at me and in a garbled voice said,

"When I was in Trona, ya know, back east in Ontario, they tried tuh hang a rape kinviction on me so I got t'hell outa there and came to little ole Gibsons. Can you believe it—I did'n do it …well, I, well I came out west."

I wanted the conversation to end as soon as possible and I vainly hoped he'd take the hint. "I think I'd better head up the coast, I've got some miles to put in before nightfall."

"There's no hurry, the boss'll be along, I'll just have one for the road," he said as he guzzled another large drink. *I can't believe it, he's an alcoholic and he's too big for me to push off the boat. Please God, let his boss come back soon.*

"Gawd, lady, you've got a helluva pair of legs." *This is getting scary—good grief I'm old enough to be his mother, I'll never wear shorts again!*

"Oh for heavens sakes…," I was interrupted by his boss who, like the Lone Ranger, arrived in the nick of time to save the day. Looking at his "good mechanic" he realized that the lump was drunk and hustled him off the boat and on to the dock where he wobbled perceptibly, then, leaning on the lifeline, gazed at me with bloodshot eyes and slurred,

"Look here leddy, when you come back down the coast come into Gibsons an' look me up an' I'll fix your engine real good, yessireee, real good."

"Thanks a lot, I've got to go now." *I'll bet he'd fix my engine—I'd be lucky if that was all!*

I made the hastiest exit possible and resolved not to return for a very long time, if ever.

But the day wasn't over yet, for after a lovely two-hour sail the wind dropped and once more I was forced to put on the engine. I went forward and tried to drop the genoa but it seemed to foul and wouldn't come down. I pulled from all angles, gently, firmly and with a jerk, but it still refused to drop. I was just a half-mile off the small community of Davis Bay where a small craft marina was visible and I called on the VHF,

"This is sailing vessel *Ern* and if anyone in Davis Bay can come to the sailboat south of Trial Islands and give me a hand it would be appreciated."

"Sailing vessel *Ern*, this is the Canadian Coast Guard, are you in a life-threatening situation? Switch to Channel 26," an authoritative voice said.

"*Ern* switching to Channel 26. No, not at all, I just need someone to hoist me up the mast so that I can free the genoa halyard that's stuck."

"Can't someone aboard haul you up?"

"I'm alone but it's all right, don't worry about me."

"Is there a boat nearby you can see?"

"Yes, there's a tug with a log boom in the distance. Don't worry, I'll figure something out. Thank you. *Ern* returning to Channel 16."

Just then a fisherman in a small boat came into sight around the island. In spite of having grave reservations about inviting another strange man aboard, I waved him over, hoping that he would assist me, and even more importantly that he would be harmless. The morning's episode was too fresh in my mind and I became anxious as the slight, middle-aged man stowed his fishing gear and slowly approached.

"I need some help, could you come aboard and hoist me up the mast? The genoa is fouled and I have to get it down."

"What, you want me to go up that mast, it must be 50 feet high, and do what? I can't stand heights and I've never been up something like that."

"No, no, I want you to hoist me up the mast, you can stay on the deck, besides it's only 35 feet off the deck."

"Oh, okay, I suppose I can do that," he said, tying his boat alongside and climbing aboard.

"This is unbelievable, you should be in the newspapers…a woman up the mast, this is something else!"

"No, for heavens sake don't tell anyone, this is no big deal," I said as I led the way to the mast where I had rigged the bosun's chair in readiness for action. Taking the genoa halyard off the cleat I gave it a shake and said,

"This is the line that should drop the sail,"

To my surprise as soon as the line was loose in my hand, the sail fell in a heap on the deck.

"What a fool, I've been trying to drop the jenny using the wrong halyard, you won't have to hoist me up the mast after all."

"Oh, thank the lord for that, I was really worried about this whole thing. I'll tell my wife but I bet she won't believe me."

He got back into his boat and headed for shore, while I continued on my way to Smuggler Cove for a much-needed rest.

Ern at anchor

During the cruise I retraced the route Charles and I had followed on our first trip to the area 30 years in the past. The scenery brought back to mind the feelings of that long-ago cruise and had a calming effect, for I found myself talking aloud to him as if he were with me. Just as when I was working on the text for the guide to the United States west coast, if I had a choice to make I would ask him what he thought about the situation and a quiet voice seemed to reply. His presence and strength seemed to be with me.

Gradually, I began to feel a sense of renewal, not in finding my old self but in discovering a new and stronger me. For the first time since his passing I enjoyed myself without feeling guilty for doing something that I couldn't share with him. I missed his company and the conversations we enjoyed, but once again I was able to absorb the beauty of spectacular scenery and feel glad to be alive. On this trip I found that the sight of a soaring bald eagle, the sparkle of the sun on the water and the peace of a quiet anchorage accompanied by the glory of good music were still food for the soul.

I met a friendly couple in an anchorage in Prideau Haven and the next day John, Mary and I explored nearby fiord-like Toba Inlet. I decided to prolong the cruise for another week, for the pleasures of the trip far out-weighed any reason to return to an empty house.

Exploring with a new found friend

I asked John about some of the mysteries of batteries and electricity, and he came aboard to check the battery connections. Casually touching the fan belt, he suddenly became animated and said,

"Oh, oh this is so loose, it's like a dirty shirt flapping in the wind. Didn't you check it before starting out?"

"No, I didn't know, I didn't think about it. How do I do it?"

I watched as he adjusted the fan belt. *That's not hard to do, I can do that.* He asked about the last oil change and I replied that it hadn't been done before the start of the trip.

When he withdrew the dipstick even my uneducated eyes told me that the oil was below the "full mark" but what was worse, it was as thick as molasses.

"It's pretty bad, isn't it," I said, remembering my days on the farm watching Dad check the oil.

"It's worse than that. You'd better get it looked after ASAP."

At Lund I arranged have the oil, oil filters and fuel oil filters changed at the marine service center. When the job was done I started following my buddy boat out of the enclosed marina and was just approaching the entrance when the engine died. Though it was a calm day, *Ern* started to drift toward the end of the breakwater. Quickly calling on the VHF to my friends I tried to sound calm but my words came tumbling out,

"John, John the engine just died and I'm drifting towards the breakwater. By the way, this is *Ern*, calling *Ellen May*."

"Put your fenders out, we'll come alongside and tow you into the channel, I think I know what happened."

What a relief to hear a calm voice and see their boat circle around and come alongside to tow me away from danger.

"What on earth went wrong, the yard just finished the job."

"Yes, but I'll bet they didn't bleed the fuel lines."

"What are you talking about?"

"I'll show you, it's easy."

John came aboard and showed me how to bleed the fuel lines to expel air that was in the system. I saw how simple this job was and how quickly the engine would die if it wasn't done correctly. I resolved that in the future this basic maintenance would be done by me, and I would be careful to do it right. This hands-on lesson not only taught me something more about engine maintenance but it also gave my confidence a boost, for at last I could begin to think of the engine as an ally to be taken care of rather than a threatening enemy. Since then I've been amused at the looks of surprise on the faces of some boaters as they see me heading to the used oil dump dressed in oil spattered trousers, and a stained t-shirt and carrying a bucket of black oil.

At the end of two wonderful weeks of rest and rehabilitation I returned to my home port feeling like a new person. A turning point in my life, this trip led me from the quagmire of grief and opened a new path for me. The exit from the black, windowless prison of depression was a door to a future where I was alone but unafraid. It took some blind courage to make the trip, but the challenge of navigating, anchoring, docking (especially when two lazy attendants sat and watched me without offering to take a line) and sailing alone had been therapeutic. I gained strength and confidence. I resolved not to sell *Ern* but to continue cruising on the coast of beautiful British Columbia.

Classic vessels in Johnstone Straight

I called a friend who had asked me to contact her as soon as the trip was over. When she answered the phone there was a distinct tone of relief when she recognized my voice.

"What were you worried about?"

"I thought you were going to do yourself in."

"What do you mean, I wouldn't commit suicide on the boat."

"Well you hinted about it a number of times and I was getting worried when you didn't return at the end of a week."

"Don't worry, I'm a new person since the trip. Besides, I wouldn't do anything to let *Ern* get damaged—I've got too much pride as a sailor. I'm okay now."

It's true, I had at one time considered suicide and had decided when the time was ripe I would jump over a 200-foot cliff just off a trail leading up to a scenic viewpoint on a local mountain. But first, I had wanted to finish off the United States Pacific Coast guide. By the time plans for a trip alone in *Ern* began to form all thoughts of suicide had left, never to return. Looking back I recognize that at the time it seemed like a quick and easy way to escape the sadness in my life. It would have been such a waste to miss the joys and fulfilling times that came later.

Quatsino Sound, Vancouver Island

16 The Last Chapter Isn't Finished

Is it really true? Have more than six decades passed since I studied foreign stamps rescued from packages of Blue Ribbon Tea and dreamed of a life of travel and adventure? Has it been over 40 years since I married Charles? Have I sailed and maintained *Ern* for 15 years since Charles passed away? The calendar, my personal journals and logbooks say that it is true, so it must be so.

I'm not the same person I was when I attended university worried about failure, nor when Charles and I were married, devastated by my parents' decision, nor when Charles passed away, and I was overwhelmed and confused. But my childish dreams and overall optimism and determination to live life to the full somehow carried me along, climbing every mountain whether skies were sunny or gray. I grasped the chances as they came along, made decisions after careful thought and always tried to leave a clean trail behind me.

My cowgirl exploits are over but I can still find joy in seeing a wild mustang galloping across a field or in watching a well-trained horse ridden with skill and kindness. Similarly, though my mountaineering days are ended, I still glory in mountain scenery and find myself looking for routes up even small rocky outcrops. Although the dreams Charles and I shared of global circumnavigation can never be fulfilled, with the help of crew I've managed to sail *Ern* to the Queen Charlotte Islands and circumnavigate Vancouver Island. The sun glinting on the water and the chuckle of a bow wave while sailing in the bay are still cause for joy. I'll always derive food for the soul from the exquisite beauties of nature wherever they are found—night passages at sea under starry skies or dandelions valiantly pushing through cracks in cement.

There is still so much to do: trips to take, books to read, stamps to sort and coves to explore. I'm keen to see winter's end and prepare *Ern* for a new season of cruising, so that once again I can head north for more adventures and the satisfaction that comes from dealing with new challenges.

'Grab a chance and you won't be sorry for a might-have been.'

Commander Ted Walker, R.N.

Glossary

Aft – at or towards the stern or after part of a boat

Beating – sailing a boat to windward by tacking or zig-zagging at an angle to the wind.

Bergy bits – chunks of ice that have fallen from a glacier

Bosun's chair – a board or canvas seat with rope attached used to haul a person up the mast using the main halyard

Catamaran – a twin-hulled sailing boat

Caulking – cotton or oakum driven between planks of a wooden boat to prevent water from entering the hull through the spaces between the planks

Cleat – a t-shaped piece of wood or metal to which rope can be secured by taking two or three turns over and under the arms

Coaming – a raised projection around the edge of a cockpit

Cockpit – a recessed part of the deck where seats and the steering station are located

Companionway – a ladder leading from the cockpit to the cabin

Conning – searching for a safe passage by visual means

Cutter – a sailing vessel with one mast rigged with two foresails

Draft – the depth of the deepest part of the keel below the waterline

Fender – a bumper hung over the side of a vessel to prevent damage to the hull when moored to a dock

Gunwale – a projection above the outer deck to impede the flow of seawater

Genoa (jenny) – a large foresail rigged in front of the mast

Halyard – ropes used to raise or lower sails

Head – toilet

Jib – a small foresail rigged in front of the mast

Kedge – to pull a boat into deeper water or a spare anchor

Keel – the lowest part of the hull which is weighted in a sailboat to provide stability

Ketch – a two-masted sailing ship with the steering station located astern of the aft mast (mizzen)

Lee shore – a coastline on which the wind blows

Lee – the side that does not have the wind blowing on it (side of a boat or island)

Leeboard – a board or canvas rigged to prevent a person from rolling off a bunk in rough seas

Monkey fist – a weighted ball secured to the end of a casting line

Painter – a rope attached to a dinghy for towing or mooring

Rhumb line – a line following a parallel of latitude or longitude

Setscrew – resembles a bolt except that the threads of the screw are used to secure the tip, instead of a nut

Shoal – a shallow area with banks of sand, mud or rock

Standing rigging – cables securing the upper part of a mast(shrouds and stays)

Step the mast – erect a mast and attach the standing rigging

Tachometer – a gauge that shows the RPM (revolutions per minute) of an engine, thus indicating its speed

Tender – a dinghy

Tender vessel – one that reacts quickly to changes in wind or water

Tiller – a wood or metal rod used to steer a small sailboat

Trimaran – sailing vessel with three hulls

Weep – water seeping between the planks of a wooden boat

Yawl – a two-masted sailboat with the steering station forward of the aft mast (mizzen)

SEND A COPY TO A FRIEND

If not available at your local bookstore, you may order through:

Charlie's Charts
P.O. Box 45064
Ocean Park RPO, Surrey, BC V4A 9L1

Charlie's Charts
P. O. Box 1702
Blaine, WA 98231-1702

Please send:

☐ A Prairie Chicken Goes to Sea
$18.00Can/$16.00US

☐ Charlie's Charts North to Alaska
$38.50Can/$32.50US

☐ Charlie's Charts of Costa Rica
$30.00Can/$25.00US

☐ Charlie's Charts of the Hawaiian Islands
$21.95Can/$19.95US

☐ Charlie's Charts of the Western Coast of Mexico
$38.50Can/$32.50US

☐ Charlie's Charts of Polynesia
$38.50Can/$32.50US

☐ Charlie's Charts of the US Pacific Coast
$38.50Can/$32.50US

Add $4.00 for shipping and handling.

Please ship to:

Name: _____

Address: _____

City: _____ Prov./State: _____

Postal Code/Zip Code _____ Country: _____

Payment by postal money order or cheque/check only.

For credit card purchases see the list of retailers on www. charliescharts.com

About the Author

Margo grew up on a farm near
Grande Prairie in northern
Alberta, Canada. While
growing up she participated in
winter sports such as skating,
ski-joring and snowshoeing
while summer activities found
her cycling, horseback riding
and stake racing. After graduation from the University of
Alberta with a Bachelor of
Commerce and Bachelor of
Education she taught high
school business courses in Alberta, Ontario and British Columbia.

 She and her husband, Charles, began sailing over 40 years ago
and their cruises included waters from Alaska to Mexico, the Hawaiian
Islands and a trip from the Great Lakes via the Erie Canal, Hudson
River, east coast and Intra-Coastal Waterway to the Bahamas. As crew
on the *Simon Fraser* she traveled from Nova Scotia via the Panama
Canal to Vancouver.

 The popular *Charlie's Charts* guides grew out of their cruise to
Mexico and was followed by guides to Polynesia, the Hawaiian Islands,
Alaska and the US Pacific Boast. After Charles' death in 1987 she
cruised the coast of Costa Rica and produced the first boating guide for
the country. She continues to update and publish *Charlie's Charts* with
regular visits to the areas covered. Margo maintains her 34' Nova Scotia
mahogany cutter and cruises the coast of British Columbia, usually
single-handed though she took crew for a trip to the Queen Charlotte
Islands and a recent circumnavigation of Vancouver Island.